ARRL's
GENERAL

Upgrade to a General Class Ham Radio License!

By Ward Silver, NØAX

Contributing Editors
Mark Wilson, K1RO
Larry Wolfgng, WR1B

Editorial Assistant
Maty Weinberg, KB1EIB

Third Edition

Production Staff
Michelle Bloom, WB1ENT, Production Supervisor
Jodi Morin, KA1JPA, Assistant Production Supervisor
Technical Illustrations: David Pingree, N1NAS
Cover Design: Sue Fagan, KB1OKW

ARRL The national association for *AMATEUR RADIO*
225 Main Street, Newington, CT 06111-1494
www.arrl.org

This book may be used for General license exams
given beginning July 1, 2007. *QST* and the ARRL Web
site (**www.arrl.org**) will have news about any rules
changes affecting the General class license or any of
the material in this book.

Contents

Congratulations and welcome! If you have decided to upgrade to the General class Amateur Radio license or are thinking about giving it a try, this book will help. Upgrading to General will open up the world of short-wave communications and a wide range of Amateur Radio bands and modes and activities — you won't regret it!

All of the information you need to pass the Element 3 General class written exam is here in the third edition of *ARRL's General Q&A*. Each and every question in the General class examination question pool is addressed with study material that explains the correct answer and provides background information. If you can answer the questions in this book, you can pass the written exam with confidence.

For more than 90 years, the ARRL has helped Amateur Radio operators get the most out of their hobby by advancing their operating and technical skills. The ARRL license preparation materials are the most complete package available. In addition to this book, The *ARRL General Class License Manual* is a detailed text reference that helps you understand the electronics theory, operating practices and FCC rules. This not only helps you pass the exam, but makes you more confident on the air and in your "shack."

If you'd like to take part in one of Amateur Radio's great traditions (and have a lot of fun, too), the ARRL provides complete training materials for learning the Morse code. While Morse proficiency is no longer required for Amateur Radio licensing, it remains quite popular with amateurs for its power efficiency, simplicity and elegance.

This book and all of the ARRL technical material and operating aids are designed to help you do much more than just pass the written exam. Visit the ARRL's comprehensive Web site at **www.arrl.org** and browse the latest news about Amateur Radio, tap into the wealth of services provided by the ARRL and look through the ARRL online catalog for publications and supplies to support any activity.

The third edition of *ARRL's General Q&A* is the product of cooperation between readers of the ARRL study materials and the ARRL staff. You can help make this book better by providing your own feedback. After you have passed your exam, write your suggestions, questions and comments on the Feedback Form at the back of the book, and send the form to us. Comments from readers are very important in making subsequent editions more effective and useful to readers.

Thanks for making the decision to upgrade — we hope to hear you on the air soon, using your new General class privileges and enjoying more of Amateur Radio. Good luck!

David Sumner, K1ZZ
Chief Executive Officer
Newington, Connecticut
March 2007

New Ham Desk
ARRL Headquarters
225 Main Street
Newington, CT
06111-1494
(860) 594-0200

Prospective new amateurs call:
800-32-NEW-HAM (800-326-3942)
You can also contact us via e-mail:
 newham@arrl.org
or check out **ARRLWeb**:
www.arrl.org/

What is Amateur Radio?

Perhaps you've just picked up this book in the library or from a bookstore shelf and are wondering what this Amateur Radio business is all about. Maybe you have a friend or relative who is a "ham" and you're interested in becoming one, as well. In that case, a short explanation is in order.

Amateur Radio or "ham radio" is one of the longest-lived wireless activities. Amateur experimenters were operating right along with Marconi in the early part of the 20th century. They have helped advance the state-of-the-art in radio, television and dozens of other communications services since then, right up to the present day. There are more than half a million amateur radio operators or "hams" in the United States alone and several million more around the world!

Amateur Radio in the United States is a formal *communications service*, administered by the Federal Communications Commission or FCC. Created officially in its present form in 1934, the Amateur Service is intended to foster electronics and radio experimentation, provide emergency backup communications, encourage private citizens to train and practice operating, and even spread the goodwill of person-to-person contact over the airwaves.

Who Is a Ham and What Do Hams Do?

Anyone can be a ham — there are no age limits or physical requirements that prevent anyone from passing their license exam and getting on the air. Kids as young as 6 years old have passed the basic exam, and there are many hams out there over the age of 100. You probably fall somewhere in the middle of that range.

Once you get on the air and start meeting other hams, you'll find a wide range of capabilities and interests. Of course, there are many technically skilled hams who work as engineers, scientists or technicians. But just as many don't have a deep technical background. You're just as likely to encounter writers, public safety personnel, students, farmers, truck drivers — anyone with an interest in personal communications over the radio.

The activities of Amateur Radio are incredibly varied. Amateurs who hold the Technician class license — the usual first license for hams in the US — communicate primarily with local and regional amateurs using relay stations called *repeaters*. Known as "Techs," they sharpen their skills of operating while portable and mobile, often

Bill Carter, KG4FXG, helps young Andrea Hartlage, KG4IUM, work her way through her first CW contact.

joining emergency communications teams. They may instead focus on the burgeoning wireless data networks assembled and used by hams around the world. Techs can make use of the growing number of Amateur Radio satellites, built and launched by hams along with the commercial "birds." Technicians transmit their own television signals, push the limits of signal propagation through the atmosphere and experiment with microwaves. Hams hold most of the world records for long-distance communication on microwave frequencies, in fact!

Hams who advance or *upgrade* to General class are granted additional privileges to use the frequencies usually associated with shortwave operation. This is the traditional Amateur Radio you probably encountered in movies or books. On these frequencies, signals can travel worldwide and so General and Extra class amateurs can make direct contact with foreign hams. No Internet, phone systems, or data networks are required. It's just you, your radio, and the ionosphere — the upper layers of the Earth's atmosphere!

Many hams use voice, Morse code, computer data modes and even image transmissions to communicate. All of these signals are mixed together on the frequencies where hams operate, making the experience of tuning a radio receiver through the crowded bands an interesting experience.

One thing common to all hams is that all of their operation is noncommercial, especially the volunteers who provide emergency communications. Hams pursue their hobby purely for personal enjoy-

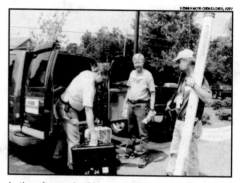

In the aftermath of Hurricane Katrina in 2005, hams provided countless hours of service. Outside the American Red Cross marshaling center in Montgomery, Alabama, Section Manager Greg Sarratt, W4OZK (center) assists David Wilcox, K1DJW (left), and David Hyatt, K1DAV, headed into the hurricane stricken zone with gear for 2 meters.

ment and to advance their skills, taking satisfaction from providing services to their fellow citizens. This is especially valuable after natural disasters such as hurricanes and earthquakes when commercial systems are knocked out for a while. Amateur operators rush in to provide backup communication for hours, days, weeks or even months until the regular systems are restored. All this from a little study and a simple exam!

Want to Find Out More?

If you'd like to find out more about Amateur Radio in general, there is lots of information available on the Internet. A good place to start is on the American Radio Relay League's (ARRL) ham radio introduction page, **www.hello-radio.org**. Books like *Ham Radio for Dummies* and *Getting Started With Ham Radio* will help you "fill in the blanks" as you learn more.

Along with books and Internet pages, there is no better way to learn about ham radio than to meet your local amateur operators. It is quite likely that no matter where you live in the United States, there is a ham radio club in your area — perhaps several! The ARRL provides a club lookup Web page at **www.arrl.org/FandES/field/club/clubsearch.phtml** where you can find a club just by entering your Zip code or state. Carrying on the tradition of mutual assistance, many clubs make helping newcomers to ham radio a part of their charter.

If it sounds like hams are confident that you'll find their activities interesting, you're right! Amateur Radio is much more than just talking on a radio, as you'll find out. It's an opportunity to dive into the fascinating world of radio communications, electronics and computers as deeply as you wish to go. Welcome!

A Question Pool Committee (QPC) consisting of representatives from the various Volunteer Examiner Coordinators (VECs) prepares the license question pools. The QPC establishes a schedule for revising and implementing new Question Pools. The current Question Pool revision schedule is as follows:

Question Pool	*Current Study Guides*	*Valid Through*
Technician (Element 2)	*The ARRL Ham Radio License Manual* ARRL's Tech Q&A, 4th Edition	**June 30, 2009**
General (Element 3)	*The ARRL General Class License Manual*, 6th Edition ARRL's General Q&A, 3rd Edition	**June 30, 2010**
Amateur Extra (Element 4)	*The ARRL Extra Class License Manual*, 8th Edition ARRL's Extra Q&A, 1st Edition	**June 30, 2008**

As new question pools are released, ARRL will produce new study materials before the effective date of the new Pools. Until then, the current Question Pools will remain in use, and current ARRL study materials, including this book, will help you prepare for your exam.

As the new Question Pool schedules are confirmed, the information will be published in *QST* and on the ARRL Web site at **www.arrl.org**.

This Book

To earn a General class Amateur Radio license, you must pass (or receive credit for) FCC Elements 2 (Technician class) and 3 (General class). This book is designed to help you prepare for and pass the Element 3 written exam. If you do not already have a Technician Amateur Radio license, you will need some additional study materials for the Element 2 (Technician) exam.

The Element 3 exam consists of 35 questions about Amateur Radio rules, theory and practice, as well as some basic electronics. A passing grade is 74%, so you must answer 26 of the 35 questions correctly.

ARRL's General Q&A has 10 major sections that follow subelements G1 through G0 in the General class syllabus. The questions and multiple choice answers in this book are printed exactly as they were written by the Volunteer Examiner Coordinators' Question Pool Committee, and exactly as they will appear on your exam. (Be careful, though. The letter position of the answer choices may be scrambled, so you can't simply memorize an answer letter for each question.) In this book, the letter of the correct answer is printed in **boldface** type just before the explanation.

The ARRL also maintains a special Web page for General class students at **www.arrl.org/gclm**. The useful and interesting on-line references listed there put you one click away from related and useful information.

If you are taking a licensing class, help your instructors by letting them know about areas in which you need help. They want you to learn as thoroughly and quickly as possible, so don't hold back with your questions. Similarly, if you find the material particularly clear or helpful, tell them that, too, so it can be used in the next class!

What We Assume About You

You don't have to be a technical guru or an expert operator to upgrade to General class! As you progress through the material, you'll build on the basic science of radio and electricity that you mastered for Technician. No advanced mathematics is introduced and if math gives you trouble, tutorials are listed at **www.arrl.org/gclm**. As with the Technician license, mastering rules and regulations will require learning some new words and a few numbers. You should have a simple calculator, which you'll also be allowed to use during the license exam.

If you have some background in radio, perhaps as a technician or trained operator, you may be able to short-circuit some of the sections. It's common for technically-minded students to focus on the rules and regulations while students with an operating background tend to need the technical material more. Whichever you may be, be sure that you can answer the questions because they will certainly be on the test!

ARRL's General Q&A can be used either by an individual student, studying on his or her own, or as part of a licensing class taught by an instructor. If you're part of a class, the instructor will set the order in which the material is covered.

The solo student can move at any pace and in any convenient order. You'll find that having a buddy to study with makes learning the material more fun as you help each other over the rough spots.

Don't hesitate to ask for help! If you can't find the answer in the book or at the Web site, email your question to the ARRL's New Ham Desk, **newham@arrl. org**. The ARRL's experts will answer directly or connect you with another ham that can answer your questions.

Online Exams

While you're studying and when you feel like you're ready for the actual exam you can get some good practice by taking one of the on-line Amateur Radio exams. These Web sites use the same Question Pool to construct an exam with the same number and variety of questions that you'll encounter on exam day. The exams are free and you can take them over and over again in complete privacy. Links to on-line exams can be found at **www.arrl.org/gclm**.

These exams are quite realistic and you get quick feedback about the questions you missed. When you find yourself passing the on-line exams by a comfortable margin, you'll be ready for the real thing! A note of caution, be sure that the questions used are from the current question pool.

Books to Help
You Learn

As you study the material on the licensing exam, you will have lots of other questions about the hows and whys of Amateur Radio. The following references, available from your local bookstore or the ARRL (**www.arrl.org/catalog**) will help "fill in the blanks" and give you a broader picture of the hobby:

• *Ham Radio for Dummies* by Ward Silver, NØAX. Written for new Technician and General class licensees, this book supplements the information in study guides with an informal, friendly approach to the hobby.

• *ARRL Operating Manual.* With in-depth chapters on the most popular ham radio activities, this is your guide to nets, award programs, DXing and more. It even includes a healthy set of reference tables and maps.

• *Understanding Basic Electronics* by Larry Wolfgang, WR1B. Students who want more technical background about electronics should take a look at this book. It covers the fundamentals of electricity and electronics that are the foundation of all radio.

• *Basic Radio* by Joel Hallas, W1ZR. Students who want more technical background about radio theory should take a look at this book. It covers the key building block of receivers, transmitters, antennas and propagation.

• *ARRL Handbook.* This is the grandfather of all Amateur Radio references and belongs on the shelf of all hams. Almost any topic you can think of in Amateur Radio technology is represented here.

• *ARRL Antenna Book.* After the radio itself, all radio depends on antennas. This book provides information on every common type of amateur antenna, feed lines and related topics, and construction tips and techniques.

Introduction

Welcome to *ARRL's General Q&A*! Obtaining your General class license opens up the full Amateur Radio experience — the excitement and challenge of traditional shortwave operation along with the VHF+ and limited HF privileges enjoyed by Technician class licensees. You'll gain access to the broadest and most capable set of communication privileges available to private citizens. Only Extra class licensees have more.

This study guide will not only teach you the answers to the General class exam questions, but will also provide explanations and supporting information. That way, you'll find it easier to learn the basic principles involved, which helps you remember what you've learned. The book is full of useful facts and figures, so you'll want to keep it handy after you pass the test and are using your new privileges.

Do You Have a Technician License?

Most of this book's readers will have already earned their Technician class license. Some may have been a ham for quite a while, and others may be new to the hobby. In either case, you're to be commended for making the effort to upgrade. We'll try to make it easy to pass your exam by teaching you the fundamentals and rationale behind each question and answer.

Reasons to Upgrade

If you're browsing through this book, trying to decide whether to upgrade, here are a few good reasons:

• *More frequencies.* The General class licensee has access to more bands. That's a lot more space in which to enjoy Amateur Radio! See Figure 1 for details of all of the frequencies available to General licensees.

• *More communications options.* Those new frequencies give you many more ways to make contacts on new modes and with new groups of hams. Your new skills are also valuable to your emergency team or club.

• *New technical opportunities.* With your new privileges come new ways of assembling and operating a station. The effects of the ionosphere and solar conditions will become second nature to you. Your improved technical understanding of how radio works will make you a more knowledgeable and skilled operator.

• *More fun.* The traditional activities of ragchewing, DXing and contesting continue to attract hams as they have for decades. You'll find that even familiar activities take on new and interesting aspects on the HF bands!

Not only does upgrading grant you more privileges, but your experiences will be much broader. You'll enjoy the hobby in ways that hams have pioneered and fostered for generations. The extra privileges are well worth your effort!

US Amateur Bands

160 Meters (1.8 MHz)
Avoid interference to radiolocation operations from 1900 to 2000 kHz

E,A,G
1800   1900   2000 kHz

80 Meters (3.5 MHz)
3500 3600 3700   kHz
                              E
                              A
                              G
                              N,T
           3800   (200 W)
3525 3600

60 Meters (5.3 MHz)
USB only
2.8 kHz
E,A,G
(50 Watts)
5330.5 5346.5 5366.5 5371.5   5403.5 kHz

General, Advanced, and Amateur Extra licensees may use the following five channels on a secondary basis with a maximum effective radiated power of 50 W PEP relative to a half wave dipole. Only upper sideband suppressed carrier voice transmissions may be used. The frequencies are 5330.5, 5346.5, 5366.5, 5371.5 and 5403.5 kHz. The occupied bandwidth is limited to 2.8 kHz centered on 5332, 5348, 5368, 5373, and 5405 kHz respectively.

40 Meters (7 MHz)
7000   7125   7300 kHz
                          E †
                          A †
                          G †
                          N,T
          7175   (200 W)
7025 7125

† Phone and Image modes are permitted between 7075 and 7100 kHz for FCC licensed stations in ITU Regions 1 and 3 and by FCC licensed stations in ITU Region 2 West of 130 degrees West longitude or South of 20 degrees North latitude. See Sections 97.305(c) and 97.307(f)(11). Novice and Technician Plus licensees outside ITU Region 2 may use CW only between 7025 and 7075 kHz. See Section 97.301(e). These exemptions do not apply to stations in the continental US.

30 Meters (10.1 MHz)
Avoid interference to fixed services outside the US.

E,A,G
10,100   200 Watts PEP   10,150 kHz

20 Meters (14 MHz)
14,000   14,150   14,350 kHz
                          E
                          A
                          G
          14,175
14,025 14,150 14,225

17 Meters (18 MHz)
E,A,G
18,068   18,110   18,168 kHz

15 Meters (21 MHz)
21,000   21,200   21,450 kHz
                          E
                          A
                          G
          21,225   N,T
          21,275   (200 W)
21,025 21,200

12 Meters (24 MHz)
E,A,G
24,890   24,930   24,990 kHz

10 Meters (28 MHz)
28,000 28,300   29,700 kHz
                          E,A,G
                          N,T
                          (200 W)
28,000 28,500

6 Meters (50 MHz)
50.1
E,A,G,T
50.0   54.0 MHz

2 Meters (144 MHz)
144.1
E,A,G,T
144.0   148.0 MHz

1.25 Meters (222 MHz)
E,A,G,T
N (25 Watts)
219.0 220.0   222.0   225.0 MHz

*Geographical and power restrictions may apply to all bands above 420 MHz. See The ARRL Operating Manual for information about your area.

70 cm (420 MHz)*
E,A,G,T
420.0   450.0 MHz

33 cm (902 MHz)*
E,A,G,T
902.0   928.0 MHz

23 cm (1240 MHz)*
1240   1300 MHz
                  E,A,G,T
                  N (5 Watts)
1270   1295

Figure 1 — Amateur operating privileges.

General Class Overview

There are three classes of license being granted today: Technician, General and Amateur Extra. Each grants the licensee more and more privileges, meaning access to frequencies and modes. Table 1 (on the following page) shows the elements for each of the amateur licenses as of early 2007.

As shown in Table 2, to qualify for a General class license, you must have passed Elements 2 (Technician) and 3 (General). If you hold a Technician license, you are credited with Element 2, so you don't have to take it again. If you have a Technician license issued before March 21, 1987, you can upgrade to General simply by going to a test session with proof of being licensed before that date.

The 35 question multiple-choice test for Element 3 is more comprehensive than the Element 2 Technician exam because you'll be granted wider privileges. As we mentioned before, the General class licensee gains access to nearly all amateur frequencies. There are no bands on which a General class ham can't transmit! As a more experienced ham, your wider knowledge will allow you to experiment with, modify and build equipment and antennas to improve your communications abilities.

Morse Code

Although you no longer need to learn Morse code for any license exam, Morse code or "CW" has part of the rich amateur tradition for 100 years and many hams still use it extensively. There are solid reasons for it to be used, too! It's easy to build Morse code transmitters and receivers. There is no more power-efficient mode of communications that is copied by the human ear. The extensive set of prosigns and signals allow amateurs to communicate a great deal of information even if they don't share a common language. Morse is likely to remain part of the amateur experience for a long time to come.

Table 1

Amateur License Class Examinations

License Class	Element Required	Number of Questions
Technician	2 (Written)	35 (passing is 26 correct)
General	3 (Written)	35 (passing is 26 correct)
Amateur Extra	4 (Written)	50 (passing is 38 correct)

Table 2

Exam Elements Needed to Qualify for a General Class License

Current License	Exam Requirements	Study Materials
None or Novice	Technician (Element 2)	The ARRL Ham Radio License Manual or ARRL's Tech Q&A
	General (Element 3)	The ARRL General Class License Manual or ARRL's General Q&A
Technician (issued on or after March 21, 1987)*	General (Element 3)	The ARRL General Class License Manual or ARRL's General Q&A

*Individuals who qualified for the Technician license before March 21, 1987, will be able to upgrade to General class by providing documentary proof to a Volunteer Examiner Coordinator, paying an application fee and completing NCVEC Quick Form 605. No additional exam is required.

If you are interested in learning Morse code, the ARRL has a complete set of resources listed on its Web page at **www.arrl.org/FandES/ead/learncw**. Computer software and on-the-air *code practice* sessions are available for personal training and practice. Organizations such as FISTS (**www.fists.org**) — an operator's style of sending is referred to as his or her "fist" — help hams learn Morse code and will even help you find a "code buddy" to share the learning with you.

Want More Information?

Looking for more information about General class instruction in your area? Are you ready to take the General class exam? Do you need a list of ham radio clubs, instructors or examiners in your local area? The following Web pages are very helpful in finding the local resources you need to successfully pass your General exam:

www.arrl.org — the ARRL's home page, it features news and links to other ARRL resources

www.arrl.org/gclm — the Web site that supports this book

www.arrl.org/FandES/field/club/clubsearch.phtml — a search page to find ARRL-Affiliated clubs

www.arrl.org/arrlvec/examsearch.phtml — the ARRL/VEC exam session search page

www.arrl.org/tis — the ARRL's Technical Information Service is an excellent resource

www.ac6v.com — a Web site that compiles links to hundreds of ham radio Web pages

Figure 2 — Like many hams, Brian Wood, WØDZ, enjoys restoring antique radios.

The Upgrade Trail

As you begin your studies remember that you've already overcome the biggest hurdle of all — taking and passing your first license exam! The questions may be more challenging for the General class exam, but you already know all about the testing procedure and the basics of ham radio. You can approach the process of upgrading with confidence!

Focus on HF and Advanced Modes

The General class exam mostly deals with the new types of operating you'll encounter on the HF bands. You'll also be expected to understand more about the modes you're already familiar with from Technician class operating. We'll cover more advanced modes and signals, too. The goal is to help you "fill in the blanks" in your ham radio knowledge. Here are some examples of topics that you'll be studying:

- Transmitting amplifier use and adjustment
- New digital modes such as PSK31
- Solar effects on HF propagation
- Test instruments such as the oscilloscope
- Practical electronic circuits
- More types of antennas

Not every ham uses every mode and frequency, of course. By learning about this wider range of ideas, it helps hams to make better choices for regular operating. You will become aware of just how wide and deep ham radio really is. Better yet, the introduction of these new ideas may just get you interested in giving them a try!

Testing Process

When you're ready, you'll need to find a test session. If you're in a licensing class, the instructor will help you find and register for a session. Otherwise, you can find a test session by using the ARRL's Web page for finding exams, **www.arrl.org/arrlvec/examsearch.phtml**. If you can register for the test session in advance, do so. Other sessions, such as those at hamfests or conventions, are available to anyone that shows up or *walk-ins*. You may have to wait for an available space though, so go early!

NCVEC QUICK-FORM 605 APPLICATION FOR AMATEUR OPERATOR/PRIMARY STATION LICENSE

SECTION 1 - TO BE COMPLETED BY APPLICANT

PRINT LAST NAME: MORIN SUFFIX: FIRST NAME: Joanne INITIAL: B STATION CALL SIGN (IF ANY): KA1JPA

MAILING ADDRESS (Number and Street or P.O. Box): 225 Man St. SOCIAL SECURITY NUMBER (SSN) or (FRN) FCC FEDERAL REGISTRATION NUMBER: 987-65-4321

CITY: Newington STATE CODE: CT ZIP CODE (5 or 9 Numbers): 06111 E-MAIL ADDRESS (OPTIONAL):

DAYTIME TELEPHONE NUMBER (Include Area Code) OPTIONAL: 860-594-0200 FAX NUMBER (Include Area Code) OPTIONAL: ENTITY NAME (IF CLUB, MILITARY RECREATION, RACES):

Type of Applicant: [X] Individual [ ] Amateur Club [ ] Military Recreation [ ] RACES (Modify Only) CLUB, MILITARY RECREATION, OR RACES CALL SIGN

I HEREBY APPLY FOR (Make an X in the appropriate box(es)) SIGNATURE OF RESPONSIBLE CLUB OFFICIAL

[ ] EXAMINATION for a **new** license grant [ ] CHANGE my mailing address to **above** address

[X] EXAMINATION for **upgrade** of my license class [ ] CHANGE my station **call sign** systematically

[ ] CHANGE my **name** on my license to my new name Applicant's Initials: _____

Former Name: _____ [ ] RENEWAL of my license grant.
(Last name) (Suffix) (First name) (MI)

Do you have another license application on file with the FCC which has not been acted upon? PURPOSE OF OTHER APPLICATION PENDING FILE NUMBER (FOR VEC USE ONLY)

I certify that:
* I waive any claim to the use of any particular frequency regardless of prior use by license or otherwise;
* All statements and attachments are true, complete and correct to the best of my knowledge and belief and are made in good faith;
* I am not a representative of a foreign government;
* I am not subject to a denial of Federal benefits pursuant to Section 5301of the Anti-Drug Abuse Act of 1988, 21 U.S.C. § 862;
* The construction of my station will NOT be an action which is likely to have a significant environmental effect (See 47 CFR Sections 1.301-1.319 and Section 97.13(a));
* I have read and WILL COMPLY with Section 97.13(c) of the Commission's Rules regarding RADIOFREQUENCY (RF) RADIATION SAFETY and the amateur service section of OST/OET Bulletin Number 65.

Signature of applicant (Do not print, type, or stamp. Must match applicant's name above.)

X Joanne B Morin Date Signed: April 1, 2004

SECTION 2 - TO BE COMPLETED BY ALL ADMINISTERING VEs

Applicant is qualified for operator license class:

[ ] NO NEW LICENSE OR UPGRADE WAS EARNED

[ ] TECHNICIAN Element 2

[X] GENERAL Elements 1, 2 and 3

[ ] AMATEUR EXTRA Elements 1, 2, 3 and 4

DATE OF EXAMINATION SESSION: 4 / 1 / 2004
EXAMINATION SESSION LOCATION: Newington, CT
VEC ORGANIZATION: ARRL
VEC RECEIPT DATE:

I CERTIFY THAT I HAVE COMPLIED WITH THE ADMINISTERING VE REQUIRMENTS IN PART 97 OF THE COMMISSION'S RULES AND WITH THE INSTRUCTIONS PROVIDED BY THE COORDINATING VEC AND THE FCC.

	VEs STATION CALL SIGN	VEs SIGNATURE (Must match name)	DATE SIGNED
1st VEs NAME (Print First, MI, Last, Suffix) Larry D. Wolfgang	WR1B	Larry D. Wolfgang	4/1/2004
2nd VEs NAME (Print First, MI, Last, Suffix) Larry T. Green	WY1O	Larry Green	4/1/2004
3rd VEs NAME (Print First, MI, Last, Suffix) JOHN C. HENNESSEE	N1KB	John Hennessee	4/1/2004

DO NOT SEND THIS FORM TO FCC – THIS IS NOT AN FCC FORM.
IF THIS FORM IS SENT TO FCC, FCC WILL RETURN IT TO YOU WITHOUT ACTION.

NCVEC FORM 605 - APRIL 2003
FOR VE/VEC USE ONLY - Page 1

ARRL0059

Figure 3 — This sample NCVEC Quick Form 605 shows how your form will look after you have completed your upgrade to General.

As for all amateur exams, the General class exam is administered by Volunteer Examiners (VEs). All VEs are certified by a Volunteer Examiner Coordinator (VEC) such as the ARRL/VEC. This organization trains and certifies VEs and processes the FCC paperwork for their test sessions.

Bring your current license *original* and a photocopy (to send with the application). You'll need two forms of identification including at least one photo ID, such as a driver's license, passport or employer's identity card. Know your Social Security

Number (SSN). You can bring pencils or pens, blank scratch paper and a calculator, but any kind of computer or on-line device is prohibited.

The FCC allows Volunteer Examiners (VEs) to use a range of procedures to accommodate applicants with various disabilities. If this applies to you, you'll still have to pass the test, but special exam procedures can be applied. Contact your local VE team or the Volunteer Examiner Coordinator (VEC) responsible for the test session you'll be attending. Or contact the ARRL/VEC Office at 225 Main St, Newington CT 06111-1494 or by phone at 860-594-0200.

Once you're signed in, you'll need to fill out a copy of the National Conference of Volunteer Examiner Coordinator's (NCVEC) Quick Form 605 (see Figure 3). This is an application for a new or upgraded license. It is used only at test sessions and for a VEC to process a license renewal or a license change. *Do not* use an NCVEC Quick Form 605 for any kind of application directly to the FCC — it will be rejected. Use a regular FCC Form 605 (Figure 4). After filling out the form, pay the current test fee and get ready.

The Exam

The General test takes from 30 minutes to an hour. You will be given a question booklet and an answer sheet. Be sure to read the instructions, fill in all the necessary information and sign your name wherever its required. Check to be sure your booklet has all the questions and be sure to mark the answer in the correct space for each question.

You don't have to answer the questions in order — skip the hard ones and go back to them. If you read the answers carefully, you'll probably find that you can eliminate one or more "distracters." Of the remaining answers, only one will be the best. If you can't decide which is the correct answer, go ahead and guess. There is no penalty for an incorrect guess. When you're done, go back and check your answers and double-check your arithmetic — there's no rush!

Once you've answered all 35 questions, the Volunteer Examiners (VEs) will grade and verify your test results. Assuming you've passed (congratulations!) you'll fill out a *Certificate of Successful Completion of Examination* (CSCE). The exam organizers will submit your results to the FCC while you keep the CSCE as evidence that you've passed your General test.

If you are licensed and already have a call sign, you can begin using your new privileges immediately. When you give your call sign, append "/AG" (on CW or digital modes) or "temporary AG" (on phone). As soon as your name and call sign appear in the FCC's database of licensees, typically a week to 10 days later, you can stop adding the suffix. The CSCE is good for 365 days in case there's a delay or problem with license processing or you decide to upgrade to Extra class before receiving your paper license.

If you don't pass, don't be discouraged! You might be able to take another version of the test right then and there if the session organizers can accommodate you. Even if you decide to try again later, you now know just how the test session feels — you'll be more relaxed and ready next time. The ham bands are full of hams who took their General test more than once before passing. You'll be in good company!

FCC and ARRL/VEC Licensing Resources

After you pass your exam, the examiners will file all of the necessary paperwork

Quick-Form Application for Authorization in the Ship, Aircraft, Amateur, Restricted and Commercial Operator, and General Mobile Radio Services

Approved by OMB
3060 - 0850
See instructions for
public burden estimate

1) Radio Service Code: HA

Application Purpose (Select only one) (MD)

2) NE – New	RO – Renewal Only	WD – Withdrawal of Application
MD – Modification	RM – Renewal / Modification	DU – Duplicate License
AM – Amendment	CA – Cancellation of License	AU – Administrative Update

3)	If this request if for Developmental License or STA (Special Temporary Authorization) enter the appropriate code and attach the required exhibit as described in the instructions. Otherwise enter 'N' (Not Applicable).	(N)D S N/A
4)	If this request is for an Amendment or Withdrawal of Application, enter the file number of the pending application currently on file with the FCC.	File Number
5)	If this request is for a Modification, Renewal Only, Renewal / Modification, Cancellation of License, Duplicate License, or Administrative Update, enter the call sign (serial number for Commercial Operator) of the existing FCC license. If this is a request for consolidation of DO & DM Operator Licenses, enter serial number of DO. Also, if filing for a ship exemption, you must provide call sign.	Call Sign/Serial # AB1FM
6)	If this request is for a New, Amendment, Renewal Only, or Renewal Modification, enter the requested expiration date of the authorization (this item is optional).	MM DD
7)	Does this filing request a Waiver of the Commission's rules? If 'Y', attach the required showing as described in the instructions.	(N)Yes No
8)	Are attachments (other than associated schedules) being filed with this application?	(N)Yes No

Applicant/Licensee Information

9) FCC Registration Number (FRN): 0012345678

10) Applicant/Licensee legal entity type: (Select One)
☒ Individual   ☐ Corporation   ☐ Unincorporated Association   ☐ Trust   ☐ Government Entity
☐ Consortium   ☐ General Partnership   ☐ Limited Liability Company   ☐ Limited Liability Partnership
☐ Limited Partnership   ☐ Other (Description of Legal Entity) _____

11) First Name (if individual): MARIA   **MI:** A   **Last Name:** SOMMA   **Suffix:**

12) Entity Name (if other than individual):

13) If the licensee name is being updated, is the update a result from the sale (or transfer of control) of the license(s) to another party and for which proper Commission approval has not been received or proper notification not provided?   (   ) Yes No

14) Attention To:

15) P.O. Box:	And/Or	16) Street Address: 225 MAIN ST.	
17) City: NEWINGTON	18) State: CT	19) Zip Code/Postal Code: 06066	20) Country:
21) Telephone Number: 860-5		22) FAX Number:	

23) E-Mail Address:

Ship Applicants/Licensees Only

24) Enter new name of vessel: _____

Aircraft Applicants/Licensees Only

25) Enter the new FAA Registration Number (the N-number): _____
   NOTE: Do not enter the leading "N".

FCC 605 – Main Form
July 2005 - Page 1

Figure 4 — Portions of FCC Form 605 showing the sections you would complete for a modification of your license, such as a change of address.

so that your license will be granted by the Federal Communications Commission (FCC). In a few days, you will be able see your new call sign in the FCC's database via the ARRL's Web site and later, you'll receive a paper license by mail.

When you passed your Technician exam, you may have applied for your FCC Federal Registration Number (FRN). This allows you to access the information for any FCC licenses you may have and to request modifications to them. These functions are available via the FCC's Universal Licensing System Web site (**wireless.**

26) Is the applicant/licensee exempt from FCC application Fees?	(N) <u>Y</u>es <u>N</u>o
27) Is the applicant/licensee exempt from FCC regulatory Fees?	(N) <u>Y</u>es <u>N</u>o

General Certification Statements

1) The applicant/licensee waives any claim to the use of any particular frequency or of the electromagnetic spectrum as against the regulatory power of the United States because of the previous use of the same, whether by license or otherwise, and requests an authorization in accordance with this application.

2) The applicant/licensee certifies that all statements made in this application and in the exhibits, attachments, or documents incorporated by reference are material, are part of this application, and are true, complete, correct, and made in good faith.

3) Neither the applicant/licensee nor any member thereof is a foreign government or a representative thereof.

4) The applicant/licensee certifies that neither the applicant/licensee nor any other party to the application is subject to a denial of Federal benefits pursuant to Section 5301 of the Anti-Drug Abuse Act of 1988, 21 U.S.C. § 862, because of a conviction for possession or distribution of a controlled substance. **This certification does not apply to applications filed in services exempted under Section 1.2002(c) of the rules, 47 CFR § 1.2002(c).** See Section 1.2002(b) of the rules, 47 CFR § 1.2002(b), for the definition of "party to the application" as used in this certification.

5) Amateur or GMRS applicant/licensee certifies that the construction of the station would NOT be an action which is likely to have a significant environmental effect (see the Commission's rules 47 CFR Sections 1.1301-1.1319 and Section 97.13(a) rules (available at web site http://wireless.fcc.gov/rules.html).

6) Amateur applicant/licensee certifies that they have READ and WILL COMPLY WITH Section 97.13(c) of the Commission's rules (available at web site http://wireless.fcc.gov/rules.html) regarding RADIOFREQUENCY (RF) RADIATION SAFETY and the amateur service section of OST/OET Bulletin Number 65 (available at web site http://www.fcc.gov/oet/info/documents/bulletins/).

Certification Statements For GMRS Applicants/Licensees

1) Applicant/Licensee certifies that he or she is claiming eligibility under Rule Section 95.5 of the Commission's rules.

2) Applicant/Licensee certifies that he or she is at least 18 years of age.

3) Applicant/Licensee certifies that he or she will comply with the requirement that use of frequencies 462.650, 467.650, 462.700 and 467.700 MHz is not permitted near the Canadian border North of Line A and East of Line C. These frequencies are used throughout Canada and harmful interference is anticipated.

4) Non-Individual applicants/licensees certify that they have NOT changed frequency or channel pairs, type of emission, antenna height, location of fixed transmitters, number of mobile units, area of mobile operation, or increase in power.

Certification Statements for Ship Applicants/Licensees (Including Ship Exemptions)

1) Applicant/Licensee certifies that they are the owner or operator of the vessel, a subsidiary communications corporation of the owner or operator of the vessel, a state or local government subdivision, or an agency of the US Government subject to Section 301 of the Communications Act.

2) This application is filed with the understanding that any action by the Commission thereon shall be limited to the voyage(s) described herein, and that apart from the provisions of the specific law from which the applicant/licensee requests an exemption, the vessel is in full compliance with all applicable statues, international agreements and regulations.

Signature

28) Typed or Printed Name of Party Authorized to Sign

First Name: MARIA	MI: A	Last Name: SOMMA	Suffix:

29) Title:

Signature: *Maria Somma*	30) Date: 04/01/06

Failure to Sign This Application May Result in Dismissal Of The Application And Forfeiture Of Any Fees Paid

WILLFUL FALSE STATEMENTS MADE ON THIS FORM OR ANY ATTACHMENTS ARE PUNISHABLE BY FINE AND/OR IMPRISONMENT (U.S. Code, Title 18, Section 1001) AND / OR REVOCATION OF ANY STATION LICENSE OR CONSTRUCTION PERMIT (U.S. Code, Title 47, Section 312(a)(1)), AND / OR FORFEITURE (U.S. Code, Title 47, Section 503).

FCC 605 – Main Form
July 2005 - Page 2

Figure 5 — When you've passed the exam and are ready to start exploring your new privileges, your radio set up can be simple or complex.

fcc.gov/uls) and complete instructions for using the site are available at **www.arrl. org/fcc/uls-qa.html**.

The ARRL/VEC can also process license renewals and modifications for you as described at **www.arrl.org/arrlvec/renewals.html**.

Table 3

General Class (Element 3) Syllabus

SUBELEMENT G1 — COMMISSION'S RULES
[5 exam questions — 5 groups]

G1A — General class control operator frequency privileges; primary and secondary allocations

G1B — Antenna structure limitations; good engineering and good amateur practice; beacon operation; restricted operation; retransmitting radio signals

G1C — Transmitter power regulations; HF data emission standards

G1D — Volunteer Examiners and Volunteer Examiner Coordinators; temporary identification

G1E — Control categories; repeater regulations; harmful interference; third party rules; ITU regions

SUBELEMENT G2 — OPERATING PROCEDURES
[6 exam questions — 6 groups]

G2A — Phone operating procedures; USB/LSB utilization conventions; procedural signals; breaking into a QSO in progress; VOX operation

G2B — Operating courtesy; band plans

G2C — Emergencies, including drills and emergency communications

G2D — Amateur auxiliary; minimizing Interference; HF operations

G2E — Digital operating: procedures, procedural signals and common abbreviations

G2F — CW operating procedures and procedural signals, Q signals and common abbreviations; full break in

SUBELEMENT G3 — RADIO WAVE PROPAGATION
[3 exam questions — 3 groups]

G3A — Sunspots and solar radiation; ionospheric disturbances; propagation forecasting and indices

G3B — Maximum Usable Frequency; Lowest Usable Frequency; propagation "hops"

G3C — Ionospheric layers; critical angle and frequency; HF scatter; Near Vertical Incidence Sky waves

SUBELEMENT G4 — AMATEUR RADIO PRACTICES
[5 exam questions — 5 groups]

G4A — Two-tone Test; amplifier tuning and neutralization; DSP

G4B — Test and monitoring equipment

G4C — Interference with consumer electronics; grounding

G4D — Speech processors; S meters; common connectors

G4E — HF mobile radio installations; emergency and battery powered operation

---

Time to Get Started

By following these instructions and carefully studying the material in this book, soon you'll be joining the rest of the General and Extra class licensees on the HF bands! Each of us at the ARRL Headquarters and every ARRL member looks forward to the day when you join the fun. 73 (best regards) and good luck!

SUBELEMENT G5 — ELECTRICAL PRINCIPLES

[3 exam questions — 3 groups]

G5A — Resistance; reactance; inductance; capacitance; impedance; impedance matching

G5B — The Decibel; current and voltage dividers; electrical power calculations; sine wave root-mean-square (RMS) values; PEP calculations

G5C — Resistors, capacitors, and inductors in series and parallel; transformers

SUBELEMENT G6 — CIRCUIT COMPONENTS

[3 exam question — 3 groups]

G6A — Resistors; capacitors; inductors

G6B — Rectifiers; solid state diodes and transistors; solar cells; vacuum tubes; batteries

G6C — Analog and digital integrated circuits (IC's); microprocessors; memory; I/O devices; microwave IC's (MMIC's); display devices

SUBELEMENT G7 — PRACTICAL CIRCUITS

[2 exam question — 2 groups]

G7A — Power supplies; transmitters and receivers; filters; schematic symbols

G7B — Digital circuits (gates, flip-flops, shift registers); amplifiers and oscillators

SUBELEMENT G8 — SIGNALS AND EMISSIONS

[2 exam questions — 2 groups]

G8A — Carriers and modulation: AM; FM; single and double sideband ; modulation envelope; deviation; overmodulation

G8B — Frequency mixing; multiplication; HF data communications; bandwidths of various modes

SUBELEMENT G9 — ANTENNAS

[4 exam questions — 4 groups]

G9A — Antenna feedlines: characteristic impedance, and attenuation; SWR calculation, measurement and effects; matching networks

G9B — Basic antennas

G9C — Directional antennas

G9D — Specialized antennas

SUBELEMENT G0 — ELECTRICAL AND RF SAFETY

[2 exam questions — 2 groups]

G0A — RF safety principles, rules and guidelines; routine station evaluation

G0B — Safety in the ham shack: electrical shock and treatment, grounding, fusing, interlocks, wiring, antenna and tower safety

Commission's Rules

Your General class exam (Element 3) will consist of 35 questions taken from the General class question pool as prepared by the Volunteer Examiner Coordinators' Question Pool Committee. A certain number of questions are taken from each of the 10 subelements. There will be 5 questions from the subelement shown in this chapter. These questions are divided into 5 groups, labeled G1A through G1E.

After most of the explanations in this chapter you will see a reference to Part 97 of the FCC rules set inside square brackets, like [97.301(d)]. This tells you where to look for the exact wording of the rules as they relate to that question. For a complete copy of Part 97, see the ARRL Web site **www.arrl.org/FandES/field/regulations/rules-regs.html**.

G1A General class control operator frequency privileges; primary and secondary allocations

If you are not sure what frequency range is covered by a band referred to by wavelength, you can calculate an approximate frequency in MHz by using the formula $f = 300 /$ (wavelength in meters). For example, to convert 160 meters to wavelength, $f = 300 / 160 = 1.875$ MHz. Remember that the values used to name a band in terms of wavelength or frequency are approximate.

G1A01 On which of the following bands is a General Class license holder granted all amateur frequency privileges?

A. 20, 17, and 12 meters
B. 160, 80, 40, and 10 meters
C. 160, 30, 17, 12, and 10 meters
D. 160, 30, 17, 15, 12 and 10 meters

C These are the bands on which the entire range of mode-restricted segments (such as phone or RTTY/data) are open to all license classes that have access to the band. General, Advanced and Extra class licensees all have access to the entire band. [97.301(d)]

G1A02 On which of the following bands is phone operation prohibited?

A. 160 meters
B. 30 meters
C. 17 meters
D. 12 meters

B The 30-meter band is restricted to CW, RTTY and data transmissions only. [97.305]

G1A03 On which of the following bands is image transmission prohibited?

A. 160 meters
B. 30 meters
C. 20 meters
D. 12 meters

B The 30-meter band is restricted to CW, RTTY and data transmissions only. Image transmission is also prohibited on the 60-meter band. [97.305]

G1A04 Which amateur band restricts communication to specific channels, using only USB voice, and prohibits all other modes, including CW and data?

A. 11 meters
B. 12 meters
C. 30 meters
D. 60 meters

D The 60-meter band is unique among amateur allocations because CW is not permitted and because operation is restricted to five fixed-frequency USB voice channels, as of January 2007. [97.303(s)]

G1A05 Which of the following frequencies is in the General Class portion of the 40 meter band?

A. 7.250 MHz
B. 7.500 MHz
C. 40.200 MHz
D. 40.500 MHz

A General class licensees have access to the following portions of the 40-meter band (f = 300 / 40 = 7.5 MHz): 7.025 - 7.125 MHz on CW/RTTY/data and 7.175 - 7.300 MHz on CW/phone/image. [97.301(d)]

G1A06 Which of the following frequencies is in the 12 meter band?

A. 3.940 MHz
B. 12.940 MHz
C. 17.940 MHz
D. 24.940 MHz

D Use the formula f = 300 / 12 = 25 MHz to get the approximate frequency range of the 12-meter band. [97.301(d)]

G1A07 Which of the following frequencies is within the General class portion of the 75 meter phone band?

A. 1875 kHz
B. 3750 kHz
C. 3900 kHz
D. 4005 kHz

C Although the 75 and 80-meter bands are part of a single amateur band, the difference in wavelength is enough for amateurs to make a distinction between 75 meters at the higher frequencies and 80 meters at the lower frequencies. General class licensees have access to the following portions of the 75-meter band (f = 300 / 75 = 4.0 MHz): 3.800 - 4.000 MHz on CW/phone/image. [97.301(d)]

G1A08 Which of the following frequencies is within the General Class portion of the 20 meter phone band?

A. 14005 kHz
B. 14105 kHz
C. 14305 kHz
D. 14405 kHz

C General class licensees have access to the following portions of the 20-meter band (f = 300 / 20 = 15 MHz): 14.025 - 14.150 MHz on CW/RTTY/data and 14.225 - 14.350 MHz on CW/phone/image. [97.301(d)]

G1A09 Which of the following frequencies is within the General Class portion of the 80 meter band?

A. 1855 kHz
B. 2560 kHz
C. 3560 kHz
D. 3650 kHz

C Although the 75 and 80-meter bands are part of a single amateur band, the difference in wavelength is enough for amateurs to make a distinction between 75 meters at the higher frequencies and 80 meters at the lower frequencies. General class licensees have access to the following portions of the 80-meter band (f = 300 / 80 = 3.75 MHz): 3.525 - 3.600 MHz on CW/RTTY/data. [97.301(d)]

G1A10 Which of the following frequencies is within the General Class portion of the 15 meter band?

A. 14250 kHz
B. 18155 kHz
C. 21300 kHz
D. 24900 kHz

C General class licensees have access to the following portions of the 15-meter band (f = 300 / 15 = 20 MHz): 21.025 - 21.200 MHz on CW/RTTY/data and 21.275 - 21.450 MHz on CW/phone/image. [97.301(d)]

G1A11 Which of the following frequencies is available to a control operator holding a General Class license?

A. 28.020 MHz
B. 28.350 MHz
C. 28.550 MHz
D. All of these answers are correct

D The 28 MHz (10 meter) band is one of the bands on which the entire range of mode-restricted segments (such as phone or RTTY/data) are open to all license classes that have access to the band. General, Advanced and Extra class licensees all have access to the entire band. [97.301(d)]

G1A12 When a General Class licensee is not permitted to use the entire voice portion of a particular band, which portion of the voice segment is generally available to them?

A. The lower end
B. The upper end
C. The lower end on frequencies below 7.3 MHz and the upper end on frequencies above 14.150 MHz
D. The upper end on frequencies below 7.3 MHz and the lower end on frequencies above 14.150 MHz

B If you look at the US Amateur Band chart in the Introduction chapter of this book or on the ARRL Web site at **www.arrl.org/FandES/field/regulations/ Hambands_color.pdf** you will see that in the bands on which there are mode-restricted segments, such as 40 meters, General class licensees have access to higher frequencies in the segment. [97.301]

G1A13 Which amateur band is shared with the Citizens Radio Service?

A. 10 meters
B. 11 meters
C. 12 meters
D. None

D Citizens Band (CB) operators may not operate on amateur bands or on any frequency not assigned to the Citizens Radio Service.[97.303]

G1A14 **Which of the following applies when the FCC rules designate the amateur service as a secondary user and another service as a primary user on a band?**

A. Amateur stations must obtain permission from a primary service station before operating on a frequency assigned to that station
B. Amateur stations are allowed to use the frequency band only during emergencies
C. Amateur stations are allowed to use the frequency band only if they do not cause harmful interference to primary users
D. Amateur stations may only operate during specific hours of the day, while primary users are permitted 24 hour use of the band.

C You should always listen before you transmit. This is especially important on bands where the Amateur Service is a secondary user. Amateurs are only permitted to use these frequencies if they do not cause harmful interference to the primary users. If your operation causes interference to stations in the primary service, you must stop your operation and take steps to prevent the interference. [97.303]

G1A15 **What must you do if, when operating on either the 30 or 60 meter bands, a station in the primary service interferes with your contact?**

A. Notify the FCC's regional Engineer in Charge of the interference
B. Increase your transmitter's power to overcome the interference
C. Attempt to contact the station and request that it stop the interference
D. Stop transmitting at once and/or move to a clear frequency

D You should always listen before you transmit. This is especially important on bands where the Amateur Service is a secondary user, such as the 30- or 60-meter band. Amateurs are only permitted to use these frequencies if they do not cause harmful interference to the primary users. If you hear a station in the primary service or receive interference from such a station you should immediately change frequencies. Otherwise you might be causing interference to the primary station. [97.303]

G1A16 Which of the following operating restrictions applies to amateur radio stations as a secondary service in the 60 meter band?

A. They must not cause harmful interference to stations operating in other radio services
B. They must transmit no more than 30 minutes during each hour to minimize harmful interference to other radio services
C. They must use lower sideband, suppressed-carrier, only
D. They must not exceed 2.0 kHz of bandwidth

A The Amateur Service is a secondary user on the 60-meter band. We share that band with stations in the Government Mobile and Fixed Services, which are the primary services. Amateurs must not cause interference to stations in the primary services, and must accept any interference from stations in the primary services. If you hear a station in the primary service or receive interference from such a station you should immediately change frequencies. Otherwise you might be causing interference to the primary station. [97.303(s)]

G1B Antenna structure limitations; good engineering and good amateur practice; beacon operation; restricted operation; retransmitting radio signals

G1B01 What is the maximum height above ground to which an antenna structure may be erected without requiring notification to the FAA and registration with the FCC, provided it is not at or near a public-use airport?

A. 50 feet
B. 100 feet
C. 200 feet
D. 300 feet

C The rules require that you notify the Federal Aviation Administration (FAA) and register your antenna with the FCC if your structure would be more than 200 feet above ground level at its site. This includes the antenna, the supports and anything else attached to the structure. (Additional restrictions apply if the antenna is within about 4 miles of a public use airport or heliport.) [97.15(a)]

G1B02 **With which of the following conditions must beacon stations comply?**

A. Identification must be in Morse Code
B. The frequency must be coordinated with the National Beacon Organization
C. The frequency must be posted on the Internet or published in a national periodical
D. There must be no more than one beacon signal in the same band from a single location

D A beacon station normally transmits a signal for operators to observe propagation and reception characteristics. For this purpose, FCC rules specifically allow an amateur beacon to transmit one-way communication. The rules impose a limit of one beacon signal per band from a given location. [97.203(b)]

G1B03 **Which of the following is a purpose of a beacon station as identified in the FCC Rules?**

A. Observation of propagation and reception, or other related activities
B. Automatic Identification of Repeaters
C. Transmission of bulletins of General interest to amateur radio licensees
D. Identifying Net Frequencies

A A beacon station normally transmits a signal for operators to observe propagation and reception characteristics. For this purpose, FCC rules specifically allow an amateur beacon to transmit one-way communication. [97.3(a)(9)]

G1B04 **Which of the following must be true before an amateur station may provide news information to the media during a disaster?**

A. The information must directly relate to the immediate safety of human life or protection of property and there is no other means of communication available
B. The exchange of such information must be approved by a local emergency preparedness official and transmitted on officially designated frequencies
C. The FCC must have declared a state of emergency
D. Both amateur stations must be RACES stations

A Amateurs are not allowed to be involved with any activity related to program production or news gathering for broadcasting to the general public unless it is directly related to an emergency involving an immediate threat to life or property and there is no other method by which the information can be transmitted. If there is an alternative communication system available, even if it is slower, the amateur station cannot transmit the information for a news broadcast or related program production. [97.113(b)]

G1B05   When may music be transmitted by an amateur station?

    A. At any time, as long as it produces no spurious emissions

    B. When it is unintentionally transmitted from the background at the transmitter

    C. When it is transmitted on frequencies above 1215 MHz

    D. When it is an incidental part of a space shuttle or ISS retransmission

D   Normally, music may not be transmitted by an amateur station. This is to avoid infringing upon commercial broadcast activities. Music is often used in communication between ground control and the space shuttle or International Space Station (ISS) for such things as waking up the astronauts in the morning. In this case, since it is an incidental part of the transmission and not the primary purpose of it, the music can be retransmitted by the amateur station along with the rest of the space shuttle transmission, as long as the amateur station has NASA's permission to retransmit the Shuttle (or ISS) audio. [97.113(a)(4) and 97.113(e)]

G1B06   When is an amateur station permitted to transmit secret codes?

    A. During a declared communications emergency

    B. To control a space station

    C. Only when the information is of a routine, personal nature

    D. Only with Special Temporary Authorization from the FCC

B   An amateur station may never transmit in such a manner as to obscure the meaning of two-way communication. The use of standard abbreviations does not violate this rule, since their meaning is well known. The exception is space telecommand operations where the commands and data may be coded. (This helps prevent unauthorized stations from transmitting telecommand messages to the spacecraft.) When controlling a satellite from a ground station, the transmissions may consist of specially coded messages intended to facilitate communication or related to the function of the spacecraft. Telecommand is not two-way communication, however; it is one-way communication. [97.113(a)(4) and 97.207(f)]

G1B07   What are the restrictions on the use of abbreviations or procedural signals in the amateur service?

    A. Only "Q" codes are permitted

    B. They may be used if they do not obscure the meaning of a message

    C. They are not permitted because they obscure the meaning of a message to FCC monitoring stations

    D. Only "10-codes" are permitted

B   The use of common abbreviations and procedural signals is standard practice and does not obscure the meaning of a message because their meaning is well known. Any use of abbreviations or codes for the purpose of obscuring the meaning of a communication is prohibited. (see G1B06) [97.113(a)(4)]

G1B08 **Which of the following is prohibited by the FCC Rules for amateur radio stations?**

A. Transmission of music as the primary program material during a contact
B. The use of obscene or indecent words
C. Transmission of false or deceptive messages or signals
D. All of these answers are correct

D The playing of music in an amateur transmission is prohibited since it infringes upon commercial broadcast privileges. Common sense, as well as FCC rules, says that using obscene or indecent words or transmitting false or deceptive messages is prohibited. So all answers are correct. [97.113(a)(4) and 97.113(e)]

G1B09 **When may an amateur station transmit communications in which the licensee or control operator has a pecuniary (monetary) interest?**

A. Only when other amateurs are being notified of the sale of apparatus normally used in an amateur station and such activity is not done on a regular basis
B. Only when there is no other means of communications readily available
C. At any time as long as the communication does not involve a third party
D. Never

A In general, amateurs are forbidden to receive any kind of compensation, financial or otherwise, for conducting communication on amateur frequencies. Amateurs are however, permitted to conduct a limited amount of personal business, such as participating in "swap-and-shop" nets conducted on amateur frequencies for local amateurs to buy, sell and trade amateur equipment. [97.113(a)(3)]

G1B10 **What is the power limit for beacon stations?**

A. 10 watts PEP output
B. 20 watts PEP output
C. 100 watts PEP output
D. 200 watts PEP output

C 100 watts of output power is a good compromise, enabling a beacon station to transmit a signal strong enough to be heard when propagation isn't the best. Similarly, when propagation is good, a 100-watt signal is not so strong as to cause interference to stations on nearby frequencies. [97.203(c)]

G1B11 How does the FCC require an amateur station to be operated in all respects not covered by the Part 97 rules?

A. In conformance with the rules of the IARU
B. In conformance with amateur radio custom
C. In conformance with good engineering and good amateur practice
D. All of these answers are correct

C The FCC rules grant amateurs a lot freedom in the ways they choose to operate, more than in any other service. It is impossible for the service's broad rules and regulations to cover every situation that might possibly arise. You are expected to use common sense in those situations where an exact rule does not apply. Your station and its operation should always follow good engineering design and good amateur practice. [97.101(a)]

G1B12 Who or what determines "good engineering and good amateur practice" that apply to operation of an amateur station in all respects not covered by the Part 97 rules?

A. The FCC
B. The Control Operator
C. The IEEE
D. The ITU

A The FCC does not publish a list of what constitutes "good engineering and good amateur practice" because the state of the radio art is continually improving. Nevertheless, when questions arise, the FCC is the agency that determines what standards should be applied. [97.101(a)]

G1B13 What restrictions may the FCC place on an amateur station that is causing interference to a broadcast receiver of good engineering design?

A. Restrict the amateur station operation to times other than 8 pm to 10:30 pm local time every day, as well as on Sundays from 10:30 am to 1 pm local time
B. Restrict the amateur station from operating at times requested by the owner of the receiver
C. Restrict the amateur station to operation only during RACES drills
D. Restrict the amateur station from operating at any time

A Imposing "quiet hours" on an amateur station is quite rare. This usually occurs only when the amateur in question did not cooperate with bona fide efforts by the owner of the receiver or the FCC. It is important to note that the broadcast receiver must be shown to have adequate sensitivity and selectivity and that interference to consumer electronics such as telephones or computers is not covered. [97.121(a)]

G1C Transmitter power regulations; HF data emission standards

If you are not sure what frequency range is covered by a band referred to by frequency, you can calculate an approximate wavelength in meters by using the formula f = 300 / (frequency in MHz). For example, to convert 14 MHz to wavelength, f = 300 / 14 = 21.4 meters. Remember that the values used to name a band in terms of wavelength or frequency are approximate.

G1C01 **What is the maximum transmitting power an amateur station may use on 10.140 MHz?**

A. 200 watts PEP output
B. 1000 watts PEP output
C. 1500 watts PEP output
D. 2000 watts PEP output

A The general rule is that maximum power is limited to 1500 watts PEP output, although there are exceptions where less power is allowed. One such exception is the 30-meter band, 10.100-10.150 MHz, where the maximum power for US amateurs is 200 watts. (These frequencies are just above the short-wave time broadcasts of WWV and WWVH at 10.0 MHz.) [97.313(c)(1)]

G1C02 **What is the maximum transmitting power an amateur station may use on the 12 meter band?**

A. 1500 PEP output, except for 200 watts PEP output in the novice portion
B. 200 watts PEP output
C. 1500 watts PEP output
D. Effective radiated power equivalent to 50 watts from a half wave dipole

C The general rule is that maximum power is limited to 1500 watts PEP output, although there are exceptions where less power is allowed. There are no exceptions in the 12 meter band, so the maximum power allowed is 1500 watts PEP output on the entire band, 24.890-24.990 MHz. [97.313(a) and 97.313(b)]

G1C03 **What is the maximum transmitting power a General class licensee may use when operating between 7025 and 7125 kHz?**

A. 200 watts PEP output
B. 1500 watts PEP output
C. 1000 watts PEP output
D. 2000 watts PEP output

B The general rule is that maximum power is limited to 1500 watts PEP output, although there are exceptions where less power is allowed. There are no exceptions for General class operators on the 40-meter band, so the maximum power allowed is 1500 watts PEP output on the entire band, 7.0-7.3 MHz. [97.313]

G1C04 What limitations, other than the 1500 watt PEP limit, are placed on transmitter power in the 14 MHz band?

A. Only the minimum power necessary to carry out the desired communications should be used
B. Power must be limited to 200 watts when transmitting between 14.100 MHz and 14.150 MHz
C. Power should be limited as necessary to avoid interference to another radio service on the frequency
D. Effective radiated power cannot exceed 3000 watts

A The general rule is that maximum power is limited to 1500 watts PEP output, although there are exceptions where less power is allowed. There are no exceptions on the 14 MHz band, so the maximum power allowed is 1500 watts PEP output on the entire band, 14.0-14.35 MHz. Of course, amateurs are always required to use the minimum power necessary to carry out the desired communication. [97.313]

G1C05 What is the maximum transmitting power a station with a General Class control operator may use on the 28 MHz band?

A. 100 watts PEP output
B. 1000 watts PEP output
C. 1500 watts PEP output
D. 2000 watts PEP output

C The general rule is that maximum power is limited to 1500 watts PEP output, although there are exceptions where less power is allowed. There are no exceptions for General class operators in the 28 MHz band (28.0-29.7 MHz), so General and higher class licensees may use the full maximum power, 1500 watts PEP output. [97.313]

G1C06 What is the maximum transmitting power an amateur station may use on 1825 kHz?

A. 200 watts PEP output
B. 1000 watts PEP output
C. 1200 watts PEP output
D. 1500 watts PEP output

D The general rule is that maximum power is limited to 1500 watts PEP output, although there are exceptions where less power is allowed. There are no exceptions on the 160-meter band, 1.8-2.0 MHz, so the maximum power allowed is 1500 watts PEP output. [97.313(b)]

G1C07 Which of the following is a requirement when a station is transmitting on the 60 meter band?

A. Transmissions may only use Lower Sideband (LSB)
B. Transmissions must use only CW or Data modes
C. Transmissions must not exceed an effective radiated power of 50 Watts PEP referred to a dipole antenna
D. Transmissions must not exceed an effective radiated power of 200 Watts PEP referred to a dipole antenna

C The 60-meter band is certainly an interesting one when it comes to regulations. There are some regulations on this band that are very different from the regulations on any other Amateur band. Amateurs have a secondary allocation, and share the band with Government Mobile and Fixed Services, who are the primary users. Amateurs may only use upper sideband (USB). Lower sideband (LSB), Morse code (CW) or RTTY/data mode transmissions are not allowed.

Amateur power limits are normally specified as a number of watts peak envelope power (PEP) output. On the 60-meter band, the maximum power is specified as no more than 50 watts PEP effective radiated power (ERP). ERP takes into account the gain of your antenna as compared to a half-wavelength dipole. So if your antenna has any gain over a dipole, you will have to reduce your transmitter output power accordingly. [97.303(s)]

G1C08 What is the maximum symbol rate permitted for RTTY emissions transmitted on frequency bands below 28 MHz?

A. 56 kilobaud
B. 19.6 kilobaud
C. 1200 baud
D. 300 baud

D On frequencies below 28 MHz, the low-frequency end of the 10 meter band, the maximum symbol rate for RTTY emissions is 300 baud. On bands below 28 MHz, the rate of symbol transmission for packet (data) or RTTY emissions is lower because those amateur bands are relatively narrow. The faster the transmission speed, the wider the signal bandwidth needed to convey the information. By limiting the allowable sending rate, the bandwidth occupied by the transmission is also limited. [97.305(c) and 97.307(f)(3)]

G1C09 What is the maximum symbol rate permitted for packet emission transmissions on the 2 meter band?

A. 300 baud
B. 1200 baud
C. 19.6 kilobaud
D. 56 kilobaud

C The 2-meter band covers from 144 MHz to 148 MHz. On the 50 MHz and 144 MHz amateur bands, the FCC rules allow a maximum symbol rate of 19.6 kilobaud for data (such as packet radio) emissions. [97.305(c) and 97.307(f)(5)]

G1C10 What is the maximum symbol rate permitted for RTTY or data emission transmissions on the 10 meter band?

A. 56 kilobaud
B. 19.6 kilobaud
C. 1200 baud
D. 300 baud

C The 10-meter band starts at 28 MHz. 28 MHz is a point of change in the FCC rules for allowable sending speeds and above 28 MHz you can use a 1200 baud symbol rate for RTTY or data emissions. On bands below 28 MHz, the rate of symbol transmission for packet (data) or RTTY emissions is lower because those amateur bands are relatively narrow. The faster the transmission speed, the wider the signal bandwidth needed to convey the information. By limiting the allowable sending rate, the bandwidth occupied by the transmission is also limited. [97.305(c) and 97.307(f)(4)]

G1C11 What is the maximum symbol rate permitted for RTTY or data emission transmissions on the 6 and 2 meter bands?

A. 56 kilobaud
B. 19.6 kilobaud
C. 1200 baud
D. 300 baud

B The 6-meter band is from 50 MHz to 54 MHz. On the 50 MHz and 144 MHz amateur bands, the FCC rules allow a maximum symbol rate of 19.6 kilobaud for RTTY and data emissions. [97.305(c) and 97.307(f)(5)]

G1C12 What is the maximum authorized bandwidth for RTTY, data or multiplexed emissions using an unspecified digital code transmitted on the 6 and 2 meter bands?

A. 20 kHz
B. 50 kHz
C. The total bandwidth shall not exceed that of a single-sideband phone emission
D. The total bandwidth shall not exceed 10 times that of a CW emission

A On the 6 and 2 meter bands, the FCC rules allow a maximum bandwidth of 20 kHz for RTTY, data and multiplexed emissions using an unspecified digital code. [97.305(c) and 97.307(f)(5)]

G1C13 What is the maximum bandwidth permitted by FCC rules for amateur radio stations when operating on USB frequencies in the 60-meter band?

A. 2.8 kHz
B. 5.6 kHz
C. +/–2.8 kHz
D. 3 kHz

A The FCC rules for operating on the amateur 60-meter band tell us that "Amateur stations must ensure that their transmission occupies only the 2.8 kHz centered around each" of the operating channels. So the maximum transmitted bandwidth of your upper sideband signal (the only operating mode allowed on this band) is 2.8 kHz. A properly adjusted SSB transmitter normally has a bandwidth of 2.5 to 2.8 kHz. [97.303(s)]

G1D Volunteer Examiners and Volunteer Examiner Coordinators; temporary identification

G1D01 What is the proper way to identify when transmitting on General class frequencies if you have a CSCE for the required elements but your upgrade from Technician has not appeared in the ULS database?

A. Give your call sign followed by the words "General class"
B. No special identification is needed, since your license upgrade would already be shown in the FCC's database
C. Give your call sign followed by the words "temporary AG"
D. Give your call sign followed the abbreviation "CSCE"

C You must add a "temporary identifier" to your call sign so that stations receiving your transmissions can verify that you are authorized to transmit on that frequency. If a temporary identifier was not used, between the time you pass your exam and the time at which your new privileges appear in the FCC database, it would appear that you were transmitting on a frequency for which you were not authorized. When you upgrade to General class, you use "temporary AG." When you upgrade to Extra class, you'll append "temporary AE" to your call sign. [97.119(f)(2)]

G1D02 What license examinations may you administer when you are an accredited VE holding a General Class operator license?

A. Novice
B. General
C. Technician
D. All elements

C Holders of a General class operator license may only administer examinations for license levels below theirs: Technician. General class licensees may participate as a VE in any exam session, but they may not be the primary VEs administrating the General or Extra class exams. [97.509(b)(3)(i)]

G1D03 Which of the following band segments may you operate on if you are a Technician Class operator and have a CSCE for General Class privileges?

A. Only the Technician band segments until your upgrade is posted on the FCC database
B. Only on the Technician band segments until your license arrives in the mail
C. On any General Class band segment
D. On any General Class Band segment except 30 and 60 meters

C You may begin using the General class privileges immediately on receiving your CSCE, but you must append the temporary identifier to your call sign as described in G1D01. [97.9(b)]

G1D04 Which of the following are requirements for administering a Technician Class operator examination?

A. At least three VEC-accredited General Class or higher VEs must be present
B. At least two VEC-accredited General Class or higher VEs must be present
C. At least two General Class or higher VEs must be present, but only one need be VEC accredited
D. At least three VEs of Technician Class or higher must be present

A All license exams are administered through the Volunteer Examiner Coordinator (VEC) system. VEs (Volunteer Examiners) must be accredited by a VEC. There must be three VEC-accredited VEs present at every exam session. Technician exams are administered by General class or higher VEs. [97.509(a) and 97.509(b)]

G1D05 Which of the following is sufficient for you to be an administering VE for a Technician Class operator license examination?

A. Notification to the FCC that you want to give an examination
B. Receipt of a CSCE for General class
C. Possession of properly obtained telegraphy and written examinations
D. A FCC General class or higher license and VEC accreditation

D All license exams are administered through the Volunteer Examiner Coordinator (VEC) system. VEs (Volunteer Examiners) must be accredited by a VEC. There must be three VEC-accredited VEs present at every exam session. Technician exams are administered by General class or higher VEs. As soon as the FCC issues your General class license (meaning that it has appeared in the FCC database) and you receive your accreditation from a VEC, you can participate in exam sessions for Technician license exams. [97.509(b)(3)(i) and 97.509(b)(1)]

G1D06 When must you add the special identifier "AG" after your call sign if you are a Technician Class licensee and have a CSCE for General Class operator privileges?

A. Whenever you operate using General class frequency privileges
B. Whenever you operate on any amateur frequency
C. Whenever you operate using Technician frequency privileges
D. A special identifier is not required as long as your General class license application has been filed with the FCC

A When you qualify for a higher license (in this case, going from Technician to General), you may begin using your new frequency privileges immediately. Until your upgraded license has been granted by the FCC and appears in the FCC database, however, you must identify yourself on the air as a newly upgraded licensee anytime you use your new privileges. The special identifier for a new General class licensee is "/AG" on CW or "temporary AG" on phone. You must send the identifier immediately after your call sign. [97.119(f)(2)]

G1D07 Who is responsible at a Volunteer Exam Session for determining the correctness of the answers on the exam?

A. The FCC
B. The administering VEs
C. The VEC
D. The local VE team liaison

B Regardless of who generated the materials used for a license exam, it is the VEs who administer the exam that are responsible for determining whether or not the answers are correct. Once correctness has been ascertained, the VEs should review the question and answer with their VEC. [97.509(g)]

G1D08 What document must be issued to a person that passes an exam element?

A. FCC form 605
B. CSCE
C. CCSA
D. NCVEC form 605

B The Certificate of Successful Completion of Examination (CSCE) is the "receipt" for an amateur showing that specific exam elements have been passed. [97.509(k)]

G1D09 How long is a Certificate of Successful Completion of Examination (CSCE) valid for exam element credit?

A. 30 days
B. 180 days
C. 365 days
D. For as long as your current license is valid

C Although your new license class should appear in the FCC database within a few days of passing your examination, should there be a delay, remember that the CSCE is only good for 365 days. After that time, you'll have to re-take the examination! [97.505(a)(5)]

G1D10 What is the minimum age that one must be to qualify as an accredited Volunteer Examiner?

A. 12 years
B. 18 years
C. 21 years
D. There is no age limit

B 18 years was determined to be an appropriate age to properly manage an amateur examination session. [97.509(b)(2)]

G1D11 What criteria must be met for a non U.S. citizen to be an accredited Volunteer Examiner?

A. The person must be a resident of the U.S. for a minimum of 5 years
B. The person must hold a U.S. amateur radio license of General class or above
C. The person's home citizenship must be in the ITU 2 region
D. None of these answers is correct; non U.S. citizens cannot be volunteer examiners

B A VE's citizenship does not matter, only whether the individual has demonstrated adequate knowledge of the US Amateur Service rules by passing the appropriate license exams. [97.509(b)(3)]

G1D12 Volunteer Examiners are accredited by what organization?

A. The Federal Communications Commission
B. The Universal Licensing System
C. A Volunteer Examiner Coordinator
D. The Wireless Telecommunications Bureau

C A Volunteer Examiner Coordinator (VEC) organization is responsible for certifying Volunteer Examiners and evaluating the results of all exam sessions administered by them. VECs also process all of the license application paperwork and submit it to the FCC. [97.509(b)(1)]

G1D13 When may you participate as a VE in administering an amateur radio license examination?

A. Once you have notified the FCC that you want to give an examination
B. Once you have a Certificate of Successful Completion of Examination (CSCE) for General class
C. Once your General class license appears in the FCC's ULS database
D. Once you have been granted your General class license and received your VEC accreditation

D As a VE, you must be on record as having passed a General class license exam or higher as shown in the FCC's database. Your accreditation must also be on record with the VEC that is certifying the results of the exam session. Those two pieces of documentation are required for you to participate in an exam session as a VE. [97.509]

G1E Control categories; repeater regulations; harmful interference; third party rules; ITU regions

G1E01 Which of the following would disqualify a third party from participating in stating a message over an amateur station?

A. The third party is a person previously licensed in the amateur service whose license had been revoked
B. The third party is not a U.S. citizen
C. The third party is a licensed amateur
D. The third party is speaking in a language other than English, French, or Spanish.

A Third party communication is available to anyone except someone with a revoked or suspended Amateur Service license. This prevents someone whose ability to make use of amateur radio was taken away from regaining access to amateur frequencies under the guise of third party communication. [97.115(b)(2)]

G1E02 When may a 10 meter repeater retransmit the 2 meter signal from a station having a Technician Class control operator?

A. Under no circumstances
B. Only if the station on 10 meters is operating under a Special Temporary Authorization allowing such retransmission
C. Only during an FCC-declared General state of communications emergency
D. Only if the 10 meter control operator holds at least a General class license

D FCC rules allow any holder of an amateur license to be the control operator of a repeater. The control operator of the repeater must have privileges on the frequency on which the repeater is transmitting, however. A 10-meter repeater must have a General class or higher control operator because Technician and Novice licensees don't have privileges on the 10-meter repeater band. A 10-meter repeater may retransmit the 2-meter signal from a Technician class operator because the 10-meter control operator holds at least a General class license. (Of course the operator transmitting to the repeater must have privileges on the frequency on which he or she is transmitting.) [97.205(a)]

G1E03 What kind of amateur station simultaneously retransmits the signals of other stations on another channel?

A. Repeater Station
B. Beacon Station
C. Telecommand Station
D. Relay Station

A A repeater station receives signals on one frequency and retransmits them simultaneously on another frequency. The purpose of a repeater station is to increase the range of portable, mobile and low-power stations. A repeater is usually located at a high elevation. This gives the signal much more range than it would otherwise have. [97.3(a)(39)]

G1E04 Which of the following conditions require an amateur radio station to take specific steps to avoid harmful interference to other users or facilities?

A. When operating within one mile of an FCC Monitoring Station
B. When using a band where the amateur service is secondary
C. When a station is transmitting spread spectrum emissions
D. All of these answers are correct

D Aside from the general requirement to avoid causing harmful interference to other licensed stations and primary service licensees, there are several specific instances in which amateurs must take extra steps to avoid interference. FCC Monitoring Stations require an environment free of strong or spurious signals that can cause interference. The location of monitoring stations can be determined from a regional FCC office. Spread spectrum (SS) transmissions, because of their nature, have the potential to interfere with fixed frequency stations, so SS users should be sure their transmissions will not cause interference. [97.13(b), 97.311(b) and 97.303]

G1E05 What types of messages for a third party in another country may be transmitted by an amateur station?

A. Any message, as long as the amateur operator is not paid
B. Only messages for other licensed amateurs
C. Only messages relating to amateur radio or remarks of a personal character, or messages relating to emergencies or disaster relief
D. No messages may be transmitted to foreign countries for third parties

C The FCC and other licensing authorities want to be very sure that the Amateur Service is not abused to provide communication that should properly be conducted through commercial or government services. As a result, third-party communication is restricted to the types of messages in answer C. [97.115(a)(2) and 97.117]

G1E06 Which of the following applies in the event of interference between a coordinated repeater and an uncoordinated repeater?

A. The licensee of the non-coordinated repeater has primary responsibility to resolve the interference
B. The licensee of the coordinated repeater has primary responsibility to resolve the interference
C. Both repeater licensees share equal responsibility to resolve the interference
D. The frequency coordinator bears primary responsibility to resolve the interference

A The FCC considers repeater frequency coordination to be "good engineering and amateur practice." As such, amateurs are expected to use frequency coordination methods whenever the potential for interference exists. As a consequence, the burden of resolving interference between a coordinated and non-coordinated repeater system falls on the operator of the non-coordinated system. [97.205(c)]

G1E07 With which of the following is third-party traffic prohibited, except for messages directly involving emergencies or disaster relief communications?

A. Countries in ITU Region 2
B. Countries in ITU Region 1
C. Any country other than the United States, unless there is a third-party agreement in effect with that country
D. Any country which is not a member of the Internal Amateur Radio Union (IARU)

C The general rule is that third-party traffic with amateurs in any country outside the US is prohibited unless specifically permitted by a third-party agreement between the United States and that country. Don't assume that it is permitted, check Table G1-1, which lists countries having third-party agreements with the United States. If the country is not listed, you may not exchange third-party traffic with amateurs operating in that country. [97.115(a)(2)]

Table G1-1

Third-Party Traffic Agreements List

Countries that share third-party traffic agreements with the US:

Occasionally, DX stations may ask you to pass a third-party message to a friend or relative in the States. This is all right as long as the US has signed an official third-party traffic agreement with that particular country, or the third party is a licensed amateur. The traffic must be noncommercial and of a personal, unimportant nature. During an emergency, the US State Department will often work out a special temporary agreement with the country involved. But in normal times, never handle traffic without first making sure it is legally permitted.

US Amateurs May Handle Third-Party Traffic With:

C5	The Gambia	TI	Costa Rica
CE	Chile	T9	Bosnia-Herzegovina
CO	Cuba	V2	Antigua and Barbuda
CP	Bolivia	V3	Belize
CX	Uruguay	V4	St Kitts and Nevis
D6	Federal Islamic	V6	Federated States of Micronesia
	Rep. of the Comoros	V7	Marshall Islands
DU	Philippines	VE	Canada
EL	Liberia	VK	Australia
GB	United Kingdom	VP6	Pitcairn Island*
HC	Ecuador	XE	Mexico
HH	Haiti	YN	Nicaragua
HI	Dominican Republic	YS	El Salvador
HK	Colombia	YV	Venezuela
HP	Panama	ZP	Paraguay
HR	Honduras	ZS	South Africa
J3	Grenada	3DA	Swaziland
J6	St Lucia	4U1ITU	ITU - Geneva
J7	Dominica	4U1VIC	VIC - Vienna
J8	St Vincent and the Grenadines	4X	Israel
JY	Jordan	6Y	Jamaica
LU	Argentina	8R	Guyana
OA	Peru	9G	Ghana
PY	Brazil	9L	Sierra Leone
TA	Turkey	9Y	Trinidad and Tobago
TG	Guatemala		

Notes:

*Since 1970, there has been an informal agreement between the United Kingdom and the US, permitting Pitcairn and US amateurs to exchange messages concerning medical emergencies, urgent need for equipment or supplies, and private or personal matters of island residents.

Please note that Region 2 of the International Amateur Radio Union (IARU) has recommended that international traffic on the 20 and 15-meter bands be conducted on 14.100-14.150, 14.250-14.350, 21.150 -21.200 and 21.360-21.450 MHz. The IARU is the alliance of Amateur Radio societies from around the world; Region 2 comprises member-societies in North, South and Central America, and the Caribbean.

At the end of an exchange of third-party traffic with a station located in a foreign country, an FCC-licensed amateur must transmit the call sign of the foreign station as well as his own call sign.

Current as of January 2007; see **www.arrl.org/FandES/field/regulations/io/3rdparty. html** for the latest information.

G1E08 Which of the following is a requirement for a non-licensed person to communicate with a foreign amateur radio station from a US amateur station at which a licensed control operator is present?

A. The information must be exchanged in English
B. The foreign amateur station must be in a country with which the United States has a third party agreement
C. The control operator must have at least a General class license
D. All of these answers are correct

B The non-licensed person is, by definition, a third-party and any messages you allow them to send or that you send on their behalf are third-party traffic. The non-licensed person cannot have had an amateur license revoked as discussed in question G1E01. [97.115(a) and 97.115(b)]

G1E09 What language must you use when identifying your station if you are using a language other than English in making a contact?

A. The language being used for the contact
B. Any language if the US has a third party agreement with that country
C. English
D. Any language of a country that is a member of the ITU

C Identification by all US-licensed stations when using phone transmissions must be performed in English. [97.119(b)(2)]

G1E10 Which of the following is a permissible third party communication during routine amateur radio operations?

A. Permitting an unlicensed person to speak to a licensed amateur anywhere in the world
B. Sending a business message for another person, as long it is for a non-profit organization
C. Sending a business message for another person, as long as the control operator has no pecuniary interest in the message.
D. Sending a message to a third party through a foreign station, as long as that person is a licensed amateur radio operator

D When the person to whom the message is intended is a licensed amateur, then there are no prohibitions against exchanging third-party traffic with that person by using an intermediary station, either in the US or a foreign country. [97.115(a)(2)]

Operating Procedures

Your General class exam (Element 3) will consist of 35 questions taken from the General class question pool as prepared by the Volunteer Examiner Coordinators' Question Pool Committee. A certain number of questions are taken from each of the 10 subelements. There will be 6 questions from the subelement shown in this chapter. These questions are divided into 6 groups, labeled G2A through G2F.

After some of the explanations in this chapter you will see a reference to Part 97 of the FCC rules set inside square brackets, like [97.301(d)]. This tells you where to look for the exact wording of the rules as they relate to that question. For a complete copy of Part 97, see the ARRL Web site **www.arrl.org/FandES/field/regulations/rules-regs.html**.

G2A Phone operating procedures; USB/LSB utilization conventions; procedural signals; breaking into a QSO in progress; VOX operation

G2A01 Which sideband is most commonly used for phone communications on the bands above 20 meters?

A. Upper Sideband
B. Lower Sideband
C. Vestigial Sideband
D. Double Sideband

A Single-sideband (SSB) modulation removes the carrier and one sideband from an AM signal to conserve spectrum and for improved power efficiency. Amateurs normally use the upper sideband for 20-meter phone operation. Whether the upper or lower sideband is used is strictly a matter of convention, and not of regulation. The convention to use the lower sideband on the bands below 9 MHz and the upper sideband on the higher-frequency bands developed from the design requirements of early SSB transmitters. Although modern amateur SSB equipment is more flexible, the convention persists. If everyone else on a particular band is using a certain sideband, you will need to use the same one to be able to communicate.

G2A02 Which sideband is commonly used on the 160, 75, and 40 meter bands?

A. Upper Sideband
B. Lower Sideband
C. Vestigial Sideband
D. Double Sideband

B Amateurs normally use the lower sideband for 160, 75 and 40-meter phone operation. (See also the discussion for question G2A01.)

G2A03 Which sideband is commonly used in the VHF and UHF bands?

    A. Upper Sideband
    B. Lower Sideband
    C. Vestigial Sideband
    D. Double Sideband

A   Amateurs normally use the upper sideband for VHF and UHF phone operation. (See also the discussion for question G2A01.)

G2A04 Which mode is most commonly used for voice communications on the 17 and 12 meter bands?

    A. Upper Sideband
    B. Lower Sideband
    C. Vestigial Sideband
    D. Double Sideband

A   Amateurs normally use the upper sideband for 17 and 12-meter phone operation. (See also the discussion for question G2A01)

G2A05 Which mode of voice communication is most commonly used on the High Frequency Amateur bands?

    A. FM
    B. AM
    C. SSB
    D. PM

C   Most amateurs who use voice communication on the high frequency bands use single sideband (SSB) voice. There are some operators who prefer the high-fidelity audio of double-sideband full-carrier amplitude modulation (AM). AM requires more than twice the bandwidth of an SSB signal, however. There is also some frequency modulated (FM) and phase modulated (PM) voice operation on the 10-meter band, but that mode also requires a much wider bandwidth than SSB. Some amateurs are beginning to experiment with digitally encoded voice communication, but SSB is the most common HF voice mode.

G2A06 Which of the following is an advantage when using single sideband as compared to other voice modes on the HF amateur bands?

    A. Very high fidelity voice modulation
    B. Less bandwidth used and high power efficiency
    C. Ease of tuning on receive
    D. Less subject to static crashes (atmospherics)

B   Single sideband (SSB) voice communication is used much more frequently than other voice modes on the HF bands because it uses less spectrum space. The RF carrier is not transmitted with an SSB signal. That means SSB transmissions are more power efficient, since the full transmitter power can be used to transmit the one sideband rather than being divided between the two sidebands and the carrier as it would be for AM.

G2A07 Which of the following statements is true of the single sideband (SSB) voice mode?

A. Only one sideband and the carrier are transmitted; the other sideband is suppressed

B. Only one sideband is transmitted; the other sideband and carrier are suppressed

C. SSB voice transmissions have higher average power than any other mode

D. SSB is the only mode that is authorized on the 160, 75 and 40 meter amateur bands

B   Single sideband (SSB) voice transmissions are identified by which sideband is used. If the sideband with a frequency lower than the RF carrier frequency is used, then the signal is known as a lower sideband (LSB) transmission. If the sideband with a frequency higher than the RF carrier frequency is used, then the signal is known as an upper sideband (USB) transmission. In both cases the opposite sideband is suppressed. Amateurs normally use lower sideband on the 160, 75/80 and 40-meter bands, and upper sideband on the 20, 17, 15, 12 and 10-meter bands. This is not a requirement of the FCC rules in Part 97, though. It is simply by common agreement. FCC rules do, however, require amateurs to use USB on the five channels of the 60 meter band.

G2A08 Which of the following statements is true of single sideband (SSB) voice mode?

A. It is a form of amplitude modulation in which one sideband and the carrier are suppressed

B. It is a form of frequency modulation in which higher frequencies are emphasized

C. It reproduces upper frequencies more efficiently than lower frequencies

D. It is the only voice mode authorized on the HF bands between 14 and 30 MHz

A   See the discussion for question G2A07.

G2A09 Why do most amateur stations use lower sideband on the 160, 75 and 40 meter bands?

A. The lower sideband is more efficient at these frequency bands
B. The lower sideband is the only sideband legal on these frequency bands
C. Because it is fully compatible with an AM detector
D. Current amateur practice is to use lower sideband on these frequency bands

D There are no FCC Part 97 rules about which sideband is used on any band except 60 meters. Amateurs have adopted the practice of using lower sideband (LSB) on the 160, 75/80 and 40-meter bands, and upper sideband (USB) on the 20, 17, 15, 12 and 10-meter bands. This practice began in the early days of SSB operation, because of some design requirements of early SSB transmitters.

G2A10 Which of the following statements is true of VOX operation?

A. The received signal is more natural sounding
B. This mode allows "hands free" operation
C. Frequency spectrum is conserved
D. The duty cycle of the transmitter is reduced

B The purpose of a voice operated transmit (VOX) circuit is to provide automatic transmit/receive (TR) switching within an amateur station. By simply speaking into the microphone, the antenna is connected to transmitter, the receiver is muted and the transmitter is activated. When you stop speaking, the VOX circuit switches everything back to receive. Using VOX allows hands-free operation.

G2A11 Which of the following user adjustable controls are usually associated with VOX circuitry?

A. Anti-VOX
B. VOX Delay
C. VOX Sensitivity
D. All of these choices are correct

D The purpose of a voice operated transmit (VOX) circuit is to provide automatic transmit/receive (TR) switching within an amateur station. The VOX Sensitivity control adjusts the level of microphone audio input needed to activate the circuit. VOX Delay adjusts how long the transmitter remains activated after you stop talking. The Anti-VOX control ensures that audio from the radio speaker won't activate the VOX circuit, putting the radio into transmit whenever a signal is received. Answer choices A, B and C are all user-adjustable controls for the VOX circuits in most amateur transceivers. Therefore, choice D is correct.

G2A12 **What is the recommended way to break into a conversation when using phone?**

A. Say "QRZ" several times followed by your call sign
B. Say your call sign during a break between transmissions from the other stations
C. Say "Break" "Break" "Break" and wait for a response
D. Say "CQ" followed by the call sign of either station

B   To break into a conversation, you will have to wait until both stations are listening so that your signal will be heard. For your transmissions to be identified during this brief period, simply state your call sign. No "over" or "break" is required, nor do you have to give either of the transmitting stations' call signs.

G2A13 **What does the expression "CQ DX" usually indicate?**

A. A general call for any station
B. The caller is listening for a station in Germany
C. The caller is looking for any station outside their own country
D. This is a form of distress call

C   DX means "distant stations" in ham jargon, so combining CQ which means "I am calling any station" with DX means "I am calling any distant station." You may also hear stations making targeted calls by combining CQ with some other specifier, such as "CQ mobile stations" or "CQ California." It is polite to avoid responding if you are not of the type of station being called.

G2B   Operating courtesy; band plans

G2B01 **What action should be taken if the frequency on which a net normally meets is in use just before the net begins?**

A. Reduce your output power and start the net as usual
B. Increase your power output so that net participants will be able to hear you
C. Ask the stations if the net may use the frequency, or move the net to a nearby clear frequency if necessary
D. Cancel the net for that day

C   Operating courtesy and common sense require that if the frequency is already in use, you should move to another frequency to conduct the net. On single-sideband phone (SSB), this means you need to move at least 3 kHz away in order to avoid interference. Net members should be aware that they might not find the net precisely on the intended frequency. Net protocol should always include a backup frequency, possibly on another band, in case the band is crowded or propagation is poor on the primary frequency.

G2B02   What should be done if a net is about to begin on a frequency you and another station are using?

    A.   Move to a different frequency as a courtesy to the net
    B.   Tell the net that they must move to another frequency
    C.   Reduce power to avoid interfering with the net
    D.   Pause between transmissions to give the net a chance to change frequency

A   It is much easier for you and one other station to move to a different frequency than it would be for the entire net to move to a different frequency. If you do not move to a different frequency to complete your QSO (conversation), the net will move instead, but this may cause considerable inconvenience and confusion to the net participants.

G2B03   What should you do if you notice increasing interference from other activity on a frequency you are using?

    A.   Tell the interfering stations to change frequency since you were there first
    B.   Report the interference to your local Amateur Auxiliary Coordinator
    C.   Move your contact to another frequency
    D.   Turn on your amplifier

C   Operating courtesy and common sense suggest that whoever can most easily resolve an interference problem be the one to do so. If you begin to have interference from other activity on the same frequency, moving your contact to another frequency is the courteous thing to do. Switching antennas or rotating a beam antenna may also achieve the same results.

G2B04   What minimum frequency separation between CW signals should be allowed to minimize interference?

    A.   5 to 50 Hz
    B.   150 to 500 Hz
    C.   1 to 3 kHz
    D.   3 to 6 kHz

B   The more bandwidth a mode (emission type) takes up, the more frequency separation you will need from a contact currently in progress to avoid interference. CW emissions require the least bandwidth and need the least frequency separation. Most radios use narrow filters for CW reception, so you should be able to select an operating frequency within about 150 to 500 Hz of another CW station without causing interference.

G2B05   What minimum frequency separation between SSB signals should be allowed to minimize interference?

A. Between 150 and 500 Hz
B. Approximately 3 kHz
C. Approximately 6 kHz
D. Approximately 10 kHz

B   The more bandwidth a mode (emission type) takes up, the more frequency separation you will need from a contact currently in progress to avoid interference. Single-sideband phone (SSB) requires considerably more bandwidth than CW, and therefore much more frequency separation between contacts. You will need approximately 3 kHz of separation from another contact in progress under normal conditions.

G2B06   What minimum frequency separation between 170 Hz shift RTTY signals should be allowed to minimize interference?

A. 60 Hz
B. 250 to 500 Hz
C. Approximately 3 kHz
D. 170 Hz

B   The more bandwidth a mode (emission type) takes up, the more frequency separation you will need from a contact currently in progress to avoid interference. RTTY requires slightly more bandwidth than CW emissions, and therefore slightly more frequency separation between contacts. You should tune to a frequency about 250 to 500 Hz away from a RTTY contact in progress.

G2B07   What is a band plan?

    A. A voluntary guideline for band use beyond the divisions established by the FCC

    B. A guideline from the FCC for making amateur frequency band allocations

    C. A guideline from the ITU for making amateur frequency band allocations

    D. A plan devised by a club to best use a frequency band during a contest

A   The goal of a band plan is to minimize interference between the various modes that share each band and use the available spectrum efficiently. This is done by concentrating different operating modes, such as FM repeaters, simplex activity, CW, SSB, AM, satellite, radio control operations, and so on into sections of a band. Band plans are not regulations. They are voluntary and are agreed to nationally and/or internationally. There are band plans for each IARU (International Amateur Radio Union) region, as well as national band plans like the ARRL's band plans.

G2B08   What is the "DX window" in a voluntary band plan?

    A. A portion of the band that should not be used for contacts between stations within the 48 contiguous United States

    B. An FCC rule that prohibits contacts between stations within the United States and possessions on that band segment

    C. An FCC rule that allows only digital contacts in that portion of the band

    D. A portion of the band that has been set aside for digital contacts only

A   Outside the United States, particularly in ITU Regions 1 and 3, amateurs share the 160 and 80 meter band with government and commercial stations. They may have very limited allocations, as well. The DX window is a section of the band where these stations may be contacted without their having to compete with stronger domestic signals. DX windows are also generally used only for contacts with stations outside the contiguous United States and Canada.

Table G2B07
ARRL Band Plan Summary for HF Bands

Frequency	Mode
160 Meters (1.8 - 2.0 MHz)	
1.800- 2.000	CW
1.800- 1.810	Digital Modes
1.810	CW QRP
1.843- 2.000	SSB, SSTV, other wideband modes
1.910	SSB QRP
1.995- 2.000	Experimental
1.999- 2.000	Beacons
80 Meters (3.5-4.0 MHz):	
3.590	RTTY/Data DX
3.570-3.600	RTTY/Data
3.790-3.800	DX window
3.845	SSTV
3.885	AM calling frequency
40 Meters (7.0-7.3 MHz):	
7.040	RTTY/Data DX
7.080-7.125	RTTY/Data
7.171	SSTV
7.290	AM calling frequency
30 Meters (10.1-10.15 MHz):	
10.130-10.140	RTTY
10.140-10.150	Packet
20 Meters (14.0-14.35 MHz):	
14.070-14.095	RTTY
14.095-14.0995	Packet
14.100	NCDXF/IARU Beacons
14.1005-14.112	Packet
14.230	SSTV
14.286	AM calling frequency

Frequency	Mode
17 Meters (18.068-18.168 MHz):	
18.100-18.105	RTTY
18.105-18.110	Packet
15 Meters (21.0-21.45 MHz):	
21.070-21.110	RTTY/Data
21.340	SSTV
12 Meters (24.89-24.99 MHz):	
24.920-24.925	RTTY
24.925-24.930	Packet
10 Meters (28-29.7 MHz):	
28.000-28.070	CW
28.070-28.120	RTTY / Data
28.120-28.189	Packet
28.190-28.225	Beacons
28.300-29.300	Phone
28.680	SSTV
29.000-29.200	AM
29.300-29.510	Satellite Downlinks
29.520-29.590	Repeater Inputs
29.600	FM Simplex
29.610-29.700	Repeater Outputs

G2B09 **What should you do to comply with good amateur practice when choosing a frequency for Slow-Scan TV (SSTV) operation?**

A. Transmit only on lower sideband
B. Transmit your callsign as an SSTV image for 1 minute to ensure a clear frequency
C. Select a frequency in the portion of the band set aside for digital operation
D. Follow generally accepted band plans for SSTV operation

D When you want to choose an operating frequency for any specialized mode such as SSTV you should follow the specific band plan agreements for that mode. Other stations using that mode are much more likely to be operating there or nearby than on other frequencies.

Table G2B09
ARRL Band Plan for SSTV Frequencies

Band (Meters)	SSTV Frequencies (MHz)
160	1.843 - 2.00
75	3.845
40	7.171
20	14.230
15	21.340
10	28.680

G2B10 **What should you do to comply with good amateur practice when choosing a frequency for radio-teletype (RTTY) operation?**

A. Call CQ in Morse code before attempting to establish a contact in RTTY
B. Select a frequency in the upper end of the phone band
C. Select a frequency in the lower end of the phone band
D. Follow generally accepted band plans for RTTY operation

D When you want to choose an operating frequency for any specialized mode such as RTTY you should follow the specific band plan agreements for that mode. Other stations using that mode are much more likely to be operating there or nearby than on other frequencies.

Table G2B10
ARRL Band Plan for RTTY/Data Frequencies

Band (Meters)	RTTY/Data Frequencies (MHz)
160	1.800 - 1.810
80	3.570 - 3.600
40	7.080 - 7.125
30	10.130 - 10.140
20	14.070 - 14.095
17	18.100 - 18.105
15	21.070 - 21.110
12	24.920 - 24.925
10	28.070 - 28.120

G2B11 **What should you do to comply with good amateur practice when choosing a frequency for HF PSK operation?**

    A. Call CQ in Morse code before attempting to establish a contact in PSK

    B. Select a frequency in the upper end of the phone band

    C. Select a frequency in the lower end of the phone band

    D. Follow generally accepted band plans for PSK operation

D When you want to choose an operating frequency for any specialized mode such as PSK you should follow the specific band plan agreements for that mode. Other stations using that mode are much more likely to be operating there or nearby than on other frequencies.

G2B12 **What is a practical way to avoid harmful interference when selecting a frequency to call CQ using phone?**

    A. Ask if the frequency is in use, say your callsign, and listen for a response

    B. Keep your CQ to less than 2 minutes in length to avoid interference to contacts that may be in progress

    C. Listen for 2 minutes before calling CQ to avoid interference to contacts that may be in progress

    D. Call CQ at low power first and if there is no indication of interference, increase power as necessary

A Every Amateur Radio operator should try to operate their station in the most courteous way possible. After listening on a potential operating frequency, if you don't hear any other stations then you should make a quick call to ask if the frequency is in use. On phone, say something like "Is the frequency in use please? This is W1AW." and then listen for a response. Many times on the HF bands you may only hear one of the stations in a conversation. This is because of the way the radio signals propagate. By asking if the frequency is in use, you give other stations an opportunity to respond before you disrupt their contact.

G2B13 **What is a practical way to avoid harmful interference when calling CQ using Morse code or CW?**

    A. Send the letter "V" 12 times and then listen for a response

    B. Keep your CQ to less than 2 minutes in length to avoid interference with contacts already in progress

    C. Send "QRL? de" followed by your callsign and listen for a response

    D. Call CQ at low power first; if there is no indication of interference then increase power as necessary

C Every Amateur Radio operator should try to operate their station in the most courteous way possible. After listening on a potential operating frequency, if you don't hear any other stations then you should make a quick call to ask if the frequency is in use. If you are using CW, send the Q signal "QRL?" followed by your call sign to identify your station. Then listen for a response. Many times on the HF bands you may only hear one of the stations in a conversation. This is because of the way the radio signals propagate. By asking if the frequency is "busy," you give other stations an opportunity to respond before you disrupt their contact.

G2C   Emergencies, including drills and emergency communications

G2C01   When normal communications systems are not available, what means may an amateur station use to provide essential communications when there is an immediate threat to the safety of human life or the protection of property?

A. Only transmissions sent on internationally recognized emergency channels
B. Any means, but only to RACES recognized emergency stations
C. Any means of radiocommunication at its disposal
D. Only those means of radiocommunication for which the station is licensed

C   When normal communications are not available and the immediate safety of human life or protection of property is involved, all of the normal rules for an amateur station may be broken in order to obtain assistance. This means that any method of communication, on any frequency, and at any power output, may be used to communicate and resolve the emergency. Just be sure you have a real emergency! [97.403]

G2C02   Who may be the control operator of an amateur station transmitting in RACES to assist relief operations during a disaster?

A. Only a person holding an FCC issued amateur operator license
B. Only a RACES net control operator
C. Only official emergency stations may transmit during a disaster
D. Any control operator when normal communication systems are operational

A   The control operator of a RACES station must have an FCC-issued amateur operator license and be certified by a civil defense organization as a member. [97.407(a)]

G2C03   When may the FCC restrict normal frequency operations of amateur stations participating in RACES?

A. When they declare a temporary state of communication emergency
B. When they seize your equipment for use in disaster communications
C. Only when all amateur stations are instructed to stop transmitting
D. When the President's War Emergency Powers have been invoked

D   If the War Emergency Powers have been activated, RACES stations are restricted to operations in the frequency ranges authorized by the Director of the US Office of Science and Technology Policy pursuant to Part 214 of Title 47 of the Code of Federal Regulations. [97.407(b)]

G2C04 When is an amateur station prevented from using any means at its disposal to assist another station in distress?

A. Only when transmitting in RACES
B. Only when authorized by the FCC rule
C. Never
D. Only on authorized HF frequencies

C No FCC rule prevents an amateur station from using any means of radiocommunication at its disposal to assist a station in distress. [97.405(b)]

G2C05 What type of transmission would a control operator be making when transmitting out of the amateur band without station identification during a life threatening emergency?

A. A prohibited transmission
B. An unidentified transmission
C. A third party communication
D. An auxiliary transmission

B This is an unidentified transmission. However, such transmission is permitted if required to provide essential communications under such circumstances. [97.403]

G2C06 This question has been withdrawn.

G2C07 What is the first thing you should do if you are communicating with another amateur station and hear a station in distress break in?

A. Continue your communication because you were on frequency first
B. Acknowledge the station in distress and determine its location and what assistance may be needed
C. Change to a different frequency
D. Immediately cease all transmissions

B Whenever you hear a station in distress (where there is immediate threat to human life or property), you should take whatever action is necessary to determine what assistance that station needs and attempt to provide it. Don't assume that some other station will handle the emergency; you may be the only station receiving the station in distress. If you do hear a station in distress, the first thing you should do is to acknowledge that you heard the station, and then ask the operator where they are located and what assistance they need.

G2C08 **When are you prohibited from helping a station in distress?**

A. When that station is not transmitting on amateur frequencies
B. When the station in distress offers no call sign
C. You are never prohibited from helping any station in distress
D. When the station is not another amateur station

C Whenever you hear a station in distress (where there is immediate threat to human life or property), you should take whatever action is necessary to determine what assistance that station needs and attempt to provide it. Don't assume that some other station will handle the emergency; you may be the only station receiving the station in distress. This means that any method of communication, on any frequency, and at any power output, may be used to communicate and resolve the emergency. [97.405(b)]

G2C09 **What type of transmissions may an amateur station make during a disaster?**

A. Only transmissions when RACES net is activated
B. Transmissions necessary to meet essential communications needs and to facilitate relief actions
C. Only transmissions from an official emergency station
D. Only one-way communications

B Amateur stations may, at all times and on all frequencies authorized to the control operator, make transmissions necessary to meet essential communication needs and to facilitate relief actions. [97.111(a)]

G2C10 **Which emission mode must be used to obtain assistance during a disaster?**

A. Only SSB
B. Only SSB and CW
C. Any mode
D. Only CW

C When normal communications are not available and the immediate safety of human life or protection of property is involved, all of the normal rules for an amateur station may be broken in order to obtain assistance. This means that any method of communication, any mode, on any frequency, and at any power output, may be used to communicate and resolve the emergency.

G2C11 **What information should be given to a station answering a distress transmission?**

A. The ITU region and grid square locator of the emergency
B. The location and nature of the emergency
C. The time that the emergency occurred and the local weather
D. The name of the local emergency coordinator

B When you establish contact with another station you should give the location of the emergency and the type of assistance that is required. It is important that your communications be clear. Try to remain calm and speak clearly.

G2C12 What frequency should be used to send a distress call?

A. Whatever frequency has the best chance of communicating the distress message
B. 3873 kHz at night or 7285 kHz during the day
C. Only frequencies that are within your operating privileges
D. Only frequencies used by police, fire or emergency medical services

A When normal communications are not available and the immediate safety of human life or protection of property is involved, all of the normal rules for an amateur station may be broken in order to obtain assistance. This means that any method of communication, on any frequency, and at any power output, may be used to communicate and resolve the emergency. It doesn't matter if the distress is personal to the station, or a general disaster. Just be sure you have a real emergency!

G2D Amateur auxiliary; minimizing Interference; HF operations

G2D01 What is the Amateur Auxiliary to the FCC?

A. Amateur volunteers who are formally enlisted to monitor the airwaves for rules violations
B. Amateur volunteers who conduct amateur licensing examinations
C. Amateur volunteers who conduct frequency coordination for amateur VHF repeaters
D. Amateur volunteers who use their station equipment to help civil defense organizations in times of emergency

A The purpose of the Amateur Auxiliary is to help ensure amateur self-regulation and see that amateurs follow the FCC rules properly. The Amateur Auxiliary volunteers deal only with amateur-to-amateur interference and improper operation. The other answer choices describe other Amateur Radio activities. Amateur volunteers who conduct licensing examinations are called Volunteer Examiners (VEs). Amateurs in charge of frequency coordination for repeaters are called Frequency Coordinators. Amateurs who help civil defense organizations in times of emergency are members of the Radio Amateur Civil Emergency Service (RACES).

G2D02 **What are the objectives of the Amateur Auxiliary?**

    A. To conduct efficient and orderly amateur licensing examinations

    B. To encourage amateur self-regulation and compliance with the rules

    C. To coordinate repeaters for efficient and orderly spectrum usage

    D. To provide emergency and public safety communications

B (See also the discussion for question G2D01.) Many amateurs also volunteer to help provide emergency and public safety communications as members of ARRL's Amateur Radio Emergency Service (ARES).

G2D03 **What skills learned during "Fox Hunts" are of help to the Amateur Auxiliary?**

    A. Identification of out of band operation

    B. Direction-finding skills used to locate stations violating FCC Rules

    C. Identification of different call signs

    D. Hunters have an opportunity to transmit on non-amateur frequencies

B Amateur Radio "Fox Hunts" are friendly competitions to locate hidden transmitters. Participants practice their radio direction-finding skills to track down the hidden transmitter — the "Fox." These skills become useful in locating harmful interference sources. The Amateur Auxiliary can use the Fox Hunters to document interference cases and report them to the proper enforcement bureau. Fox hunts also make everyone aware that there is a plan in place to find and eliminate an interference source.

G2D04 **What is an azimuthal projection map?**

A. A world map projection centered on the North Pole
B. A world map projection centered on a particular location
C. A world map that shows the angle at which an amateur satellite crosses the equator
D. A world map that shows the number of degrees longitude that an amateur satellite appears to move westward at the equator with each orbit

B An azimuthal map, or azimuthal-equidistant projection map, is also called a great circle map. When this type of map is centered on your location, a straight line is equivalent to stretching a string between two points on a globe. That line gives you the shortest distance between two points. This type of map is used for determining the direction to point your antenna for short-path communication. (A compass bearing 180 degrees different from the short-path direction will indicate the direction to point your antenna for long-path communication.)

Figure G2-1 — This azimuthal equidistant world map is centered on the central United States.

G2D05 What is the most useful type of map to use when orienting a
directional HF antenna toward a distant station?

A. Azimuthal projection
B. Mercator projection
C. Polar projection
D. Stereographic projection

A An azimuthal map, or azimuthal-equidistant projection map, is also called a
great circle map. When this type of map is centered on your location, a straight
line is equivalent to stretching a string between two points on a globe, and will
give you the shortest distance between two points. This type of map is used for
orienting a directional HF antenna toward a distant station.

**Figure G2-2 — This azimuthal equidistant world map shows how an amateur in
central United States would point a beam antenna for a contact with a station in
Cape Town, South Africa.**

G2D06 How is a directional antenna pointed when making a "long path" contact with another station?

- A. Toward the rising sun
- B. Along the Gray Line
- C. 180 degrees from its short-path heading
- D. Toward the North

C The shortest direct route, or great-circle path between two points, is called the short path. If a directional antenna is pointed in exactly the opposite direction, 180 degrees different from the short-path direction, communication can be attempted on the long path. Long-path communication may be available when the more direct short path is closed. Because of the higher number of hops required, long path often works best when the path is across the ocean, a good reflector of HF signals.

Figure G2-3 — This azimuthal equidistant world map shows how W1AW in Newington, Connecticut would point a beam antenna to make a long-path contact with Tokyo, Japan or Perth, Australia. Notice that the paths in both cases lie almost entirely over water, rather than over land masses.

G2D07 Which of the following information must a licensee retain as part of their station records?

A. The call sign of other amateurs operating your station
B. Antenna gain calculations or manufacturer's data for antennas used on 60 meters
C. A record of all contacts made with stations in foreign countries
D. A copy of all third party messages sent through your station

B FCC rules require that you maintain a record of antenna gain for operations on 60 meters if you use an antenna other than a dipole. You may measure or calculate antenna gain or cite manufacturer's data. (See also the discussion for questions G2D08 and G2D12.) [97.303(s)]

G2D08 Why do many amateurs keep a log even though the FCC doesn't require it?

A. The ITU requires a log of all international contacts
B. The ITU requires a log of all international third party traffic
C. The log provides evidence of operation needed to renew a license without retest
D. To help with a reply if FCC requests information on who was control operator of your station at a given date and time

D While useful, the FCC does not require you to keep a record (log) of your transmissions. It can be fun to keep a log, though, and then look back years later at the contacts you made. A log can also help document when your station was on the air and who was the control operator. You must give permission before a visiting amateur may operate your station. If you designate another amateur to be the control operator of your station, you both share the responsibility for the proper operation of the station. Unless your station records (log) show otherwise, the FCC will assume you were the control operator any time your station was operated. [97.103(b)]

G2D09 What information is traditionally contained in a station log?

A. Date and time of contact
B. Band and/or frequency of the contact
C. Call sign of station contacted and the signal report given
D. All of these choices are correct

D You can keep any information in your log that you would like to remember later. At a minimum, most amateurs keep a record of the date and time of each contact as well as the frequency or band of the contact. The station call sign and the RST signal report given and received are also normally recorded. Many amateurs also record the name of the other operator as well as his or her location.

G2D10 **What is QRP operation?**

A. Remote Piloted Model control
B. Low power transmit operation, usually about 5 watts
C. Transmission using Quick Response Protocol
D. Traffic Relay Procedure net operation

B   QRP is a Q-signal that means "lower your transmitter power." Many amateurs enjoy using low power levels for the challenge, the relative simplicity of the equipment, and sometimes to reduce interference. The generally accepted level for "QRP" power is 5 watts of transmitter output.

G2D11 **Which HF antenna would be the best to use for minimizing interference?**

A. A bi-directional antenna
B. An isotropic antenna
C. A unidirectional antenna
D. An omnidirectional antenna

C   Most of the time we think about using a beam antenna to send more of our transmitted power toward the desired station. A beam antenna can also be an effective tool for fighting received interference. For example, you might be having a conversation with another amateur, but a strong signal from a station on a nearby frequency is causing a bit of interference. With a beam antenna you might be able to turn the antenna so the interfering station is off the side or back of your antenna. In that case the antenna will not receive as strong a signal from the interfering station. Ideally, you would have an antenna that sends and receives signals in one direction, while rejecting signals in all other directions. This is called a unidirectional antenna. Most Yagi antennas will still send and receive some signal off the back and sides of the antenna, but it will be significantly less than the amount that is sent and received from the front of the antenna.

G2D12 Which of the following is required by the FCC rules when operating in the 60 meter band?

A. If you are using other than a dipole antenna, you must keep a record of the gain of your antenna
B. You must keep a log of the date, time, frequency, power level and stations worked
C. You must keep a log of all third party traffic
D. You must keep a log of the manufacturer of your equipment and the antenna used

A The FCC rules for operating on the amateur 60-meter band are quite different from the rules for any other amateur band. One significant difference is the requirement to transmit with no more than 50 watts effective radiated power (ERP). ERP is a measurement of power as compared to that radiated from a dipole. If you are using a half-wavelength dipole antenna, you can use up to 50 W PEP from your transmitter on that band. If you are using an antenna that has some gain compared to a dipole, then you will have to reduce your transmitter power accordingly. If the antenna has a gain of 3 dBd (3 dB compared to a dipole) then you would have to reduce transmitter power by half (to 25 W PEP). The FCC requires you to keep a record of your antenna gain, if it is more than a dipole. This record can either be from the manufacturer's data, from calculations of the gain or from gain measurements. [97.303(s)]

G2E Digital operating: procedures, procedural signals and common abbreviations

G2E01 Which mode should be selected when using a SSB transmitter with an Audio Frequency Shift Keying (AFSK) RTTY signal?

A. USB
B. DSB
C. CW
D. LSB

D Lower sideband (LSB) is used by convention for AFSK RTTY signals on all bands. There is no technical reason why LSB is preferred over USB for RTTY signals.

G2E02   How many data bits are sent in a single PSK31 character?

- A. The number varies
- B. 5
- C. 7
- D. 8

A   One of the interesting properties of the PSK31 mode is that it uses a character code called Varicode. Developed by Peter Martinez, G3PLX, Varicode uses shorter character lengths for the more common characters, and longer codes for less common characters. Thus, the number of data bits per character depends on which character is being sent. This is quite different from other digital modes that have fixed-length codes. For example, every Baudot RTTY character has five data bits.

G2E03   What part of a data packet contains the routing and handling information?

- A. Directory
- B. Preamble
- C. Header
- D. Footer

C   Packet radio gets its name from the concept of breaking the information to be transmitted into small pieces, called packets. Each packet can be transmitted and make its way through the network independently. The entire message is then reassembled at the receiving station. Each packet consists of a header that contains several sets (fields) of information about the packet. The address field of the header contains information about the station for whom the message is intended, the sending station and possibly specific relay stations. A control field contains information about the type of data being sent. A frame number allows the receiving station reassemble the entire message in order. The data field of the packet contains the actual data being sent. After the data field there is a frame check sequence (FCS) or cyclic redundancy check (CRC) field that is used for error detection. If both the sending and receiving station calculate the same FCS or CRC, the receiving station acknowledges the packet frame as having been received correctly. If the packet is not acknowledged within the specified time limit, the sending station will send that packet again.

G2E04 Which of the following 20 meter band segments is most often used for most data transmissions?

A. 14.000 - 14.050 MHz
B. 14.070 - 14.100 MHz
C. 14.150 - 14.225 MHz
D. 14.275 - 14.350 MHz

B The FCC's rules specify where RTTY and data transmissions are allowed, but the band plans tell you where such signals are usually found. The band plan calls for RTTY and data operation from 14.070 to 14.095 MHz on 20 meters.

Table G2E04
ARRL Band Plan for RTTY/Data Frequencies

Band (Meters)	RTTY/Data Frequencies (MHz)
160	1.800 - 1.810
80	3.570 - 3.600
40	7.080 - 7.125
30	10.130 - 10.140
20	14.070 - 14.095
17	18.100 - 18.105
15	21.070 - 21.110
12	24.920 - 24.925
10	28.070 - 28.120

G2E05 Which of the following describes Baudot RTTY?

A. 7-bit code, with start, stop and parity bits
B. Utilizes error detection and correction
C. 5-bit code, with additional start and stop bits
D. Two major operating modes are SELCAL and LISTEN

C The radioteletype (RTTY) Baudot code uses five data bits per character. This means there are only 32 possible character combinations. The code only transmits upper case letters. "LTRS" and "FIGS" characters select the alphabet table or a numbers and punctuation table to provide additional characters. Baudot RTTY is an asynchronous communication mode, so each character must also include a start and a stop bit.

G2E06 **What is the most common frequency shift for RTTY emissions in the amateur HF bands?**

A. 85 Hz
B. 170 Hz
C. 425 Hz
D. 850 Hz

B RTTY operation on the HF bands uses frequency-shift keying (FSK) to convey the information. The transmitted signal shifts between two frequencies, called the MARK and SPACE frequencies. The two frequencies used are normally 170 Hz apart for HF communication.

G2E07 **What does the abbreviation "RTTY" stand for?**

A. "Returning To You", meaning "your turn to transmit"
B. Radio-Teletype
C. A general call to all digital stations
D. Repeater Transmission Type

B RTTY stands for radioteletype. The official name for RTTY is narrow-band, direct printing telegraphy.

G2E08 **What segment of the 80 meter band is most commonly used for data transmissions?**

A. 3570 - 3600 kHz
B. 3500 - 3525 kHz
C. 3700 - 3750 kHz
D. 3775 - 3825 kHz

A The FCC's rules specify where RTTY and data transmissions are allowed, but the band plans tell you where such signals are usually found. The band plan calls for RTTY operation from 3570 to 3600 kHz on 80 meters. See the band plans in the explanation for question G2E04.

G2E09 **Where are PSK signals generally found on the 20 meter band?**

A. In the low end of the phone band
B. In the high end of the phone band
C. In the weak signal portion of the band
D. Around 14.070 MHz

D PSK signals are generally found in the vicinity of 14.070 MHz on the 20 meter band. See the band plans in the explanation for question G2E04.

G2E10 What is a major advantage of MFSK16 compared to other digital modes?

A. It is much higher speed than RTTY
B. It is much narrower bandwidth than most digital modes
C. It has built-in error correction
D. It offers good performance in weak signal environment without error correction

D MFSK16 stands for Multi-Frequency Shift Keying with 16 different tones being transmitted. On the air, an MFSK16 signals sounds like a set of whistles all being played simultaneously in a narrow bandwidth. By carefully shaping the signal and controlling how the tones are turned on and off, MFSK16 modulation is able to better withstand the fading and distortion associated with sky-wave signals.

G2E11 What does the abbreviation "MFSK" stand for?

A. Manual Frequency Shift Keying
B. Multi (or Multiple) Frequency Shift Keying
C. Manual Frequency Sideband Keying
D. Multi (or Multiple) Frequency Sideband Keying

B See the explanation for question G2E10.

G2F CW operating procedures and procedural signals, Q signals and common abbreviations; full break in

G2F01 Which of the following describes full break-in telegraphy (QSK)?

A. Breaking stations send the Morse code prosign BK
B. Automatic keyers are used to send Morse code instead of hand keys
C. An operator must activate a manual send/receive switch before and after every transmission
D. Incoming signals are received between transmitted code character elements

D Full break-in telegraphy allows you to receive signals between your transmitted Morse code dots and dashes and between words. The advantage is that if you are sending message traffic, the receiving station can send back to you (break in) and stop you for repeats of missed words. QSK is the Q signal used to describe this type of operation.

G2F02   **What should you do if a CW station sends "QRS" when using Morse code?**

A. Send slower
B. Change frequency
C. Increase your power
D. Repeat everything twice

A   QRS is the Q-signal that means "Send slower." To ask if you should send slower, send QRS? Conversely, to increase speed, QRQ is used.

G2F03   **What does it mean when a CW operator sends "KN" at the end of a transmission?**

A. Listening for novice stations
B. Operating full break-in
C. Listening only for a specific station or stations
D. Closing station now

C   KN is an example of a CW prosign, procedural signals that help coordinate the exchange of messages and the beginning and ending of transmissions. The patterns of dots and dashes that make up prosigns are described by a pair of regular letters that, if sent together without a pause, are equivalent to the prosign. The prosign $\overline{KN}$ means that only the specific station called should respond. The overscore means that the letters K and N are sent together without a space between them.

G2F04   **What does it mean when a CW operator sends "CL" at the end of a transmission?**

A. Keep frequency clear
B. Operating full break-in
C. Listening only for a specific station or stations
D. Closing station

D   CL means "I am closing the station (leaving the air) after this transmission."

G2F05   **What is the best speed to use answering a CQ in Morse Code?**

A. The speed at which you are most comfortable copying
B. The speed at which the CQ was sent
C. A slow speed until contact is established
D. 5 wpm, as all operators licensed to operate CW can copy this speed

B   An operator calling CQ is assumed to be sending at a speed at which he or she feels comfortable receiving. Responding at a significantly higher speed is impolite and may be embarrassing to the other operator if they are unable to copy your response. If you are uncomfortable responding at the sending station's speed, send at the highest rate at which you are comfortable receiving. It is good practice to respond to calling stations at their sending speed, if it is significantly slower.

G2F06 **What does the term "zero beat" mean in CW operation?**

A. Matching the speed of the transmitting station
B. Operating split to avoid interference on frequency
C. Sending without error
D. Matching the frequency of the transmitting station

D Zero beat means to match the frequency of the transmitting station. When separate receivers and transmitters were the norm, a transmitter's frequency had to be adjusted to match the received signal's frequency. This was done by spotting — turning on the transmitter's low power stages and listening for that signal in the receiver. When the beat frequency between the desired signal and the transmitter's spotting signal reached zero frequency or zero beat, the transmitter signal and the received signal were on matching frequencies.

G2F07 **When sending CW, what does a "C" mean when added to the RST report?**

A. Chirpy or unstable signal
B. Report was read from S meter reading rather than estimated
C. 100 percent copy
D. Key clicks

A An RST with "C" appended, such as 579C, indicates that the signal is being received with chirp, a short frequency shift as the transmitter stabilizes after keying. It's a very distinctive sound and is caused by the transmitter's oscillator changing frequency when the key is closed. This can be from a problem with the oscillator circuit design, but is usually caused by poor regulation of the power supply.

G2F08 **What prosign is sent using CW to indicate the end of a formal message?**

A. SK
B. BK
C. AR
D. KN

C The National Traffic System has established specific procedures for passing formal written messages by Amateur Radio. Even if you don't participate in traffic nets, it is a good idea to be familiar with the procedures for handling such messages. It can be especially helpful in an emergency for a number of reasons. By following the standard procedures it is more likely that an emergency message will be transmitted (and received) correctly. When sending formal messages using Morse code (CW), you send the message preamble, name and address, message body and signature. To indicate that this is the end of the message, send the CW procedural signal (prosign) $\overline{AR}$ to show clearly that all the information has been sent. When the receiving station has accurately recorded the entire message, they will acknowledge receipt of the message by sending "QSL" or simply "R" for "received." (See also the discussion for G2F03.)

G2F09 What does the Q signal "QSL" mean when operating CW?

    A. Send slower

    B. We have already confirmed by card

    C. I acknowledge receipt

    D. We have worked before

C   QSL is the Q-signal that means "I acknowledge receipt." Informally, it is often used to indicate that a transmission was received and understood. QSL cards are exchanged to confirm that a contact was made.

G2F10 What does the Q signal "QRQ" mean when operating CW?

    A. Slow down

    B. Send faster

    C. Zero beat my signal

    D. Quitting operation

B   See the discussion for question G2F02.

G2F11 What does the Q signal "QRV" mean when operating CW?

    A. You are sending too fast

    B. There is interference on the frequency

    C. I am quitting for the day

    D. I am ready to receive messages

D   QRV is the Q-signal that means "I am ready to copy" and indicates that the station with the message may begin transmitting. QRV is used whether the message is formal traffic or just regular conversation.

Radio Wave Propagation

Your General class exam (Element 3) will consist of 35 questions taken from the General class question pool as prepared by the Volunteer Examiner Coordinators' Question Pool Committee. A certain number of questions are taken from each of the 10 subelements. There will be 3 questions from the subelement shown in this chapter. These questions are divided into 3 groups, labeled G3A through G3C.

G3A Sunspots and solar radiation; ionospheric disturbances; propagation forecasting and indices

G3A01   What can be done at an amateur station to continue communications during a sudden ionospheric disturbance?

A. Try a higher frequency
B. Try the other sideband
C. Try a different antenna polarization
D. Try a different frequency shift

A   A sudden ionospheric disturbance (SID) is often the result of solar flares that release large amounts of radiation. Ultraviolet and X-ray radiation from the Sun travels at the speed of light, reaching the Earth in about eight minutes. When this radiation reaches the Earth, the level of ionization in the ionosphere increases rapidly. This causes D-layer absorption of radio waves to increase significantly. Since lower frequencies are affected more by absorption than higher frequencies, try moving to a higher frequency band to continue communication.

G3A02 **What effect does a Sudden Ionospheric Disturbance (SID) have on the daytime ionospheric propagation of HF radio waves?**

A. It disrupts higher-latitude paths more than lower-latitude paths
B. It disrupts signals on lower frequencies more than those on higher frequencies
C. It disrupts communications via satellite more than direct communications
D. None, only areas on the night side of the Earth are affected

B (See also the discussion for question G3A01.) Absorption of radio signals in the D-layer is always stronger at lower frequencies. When an SID occurs, D-layer ionization increases, affecting lower frequency signals more than higher frequency signals.

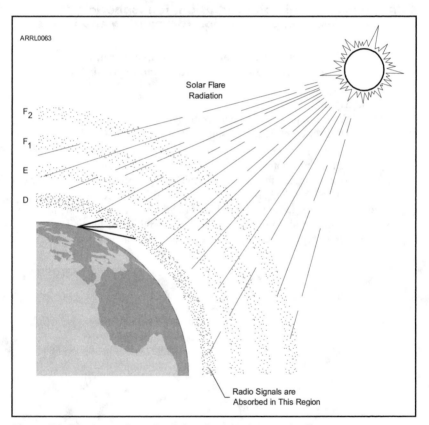

Figure G3-1 — Approximately eight minutes after a solar flare occurs on the Sun, the ultraviolet and X-ray radiation released by the flare reaches the Earth. This radiation causes increased ionization and radio-wave absorption in the D region of the ionosphere.

G3A03 How long does it take the increased ultraviolet and X-ray radiation from solar flares to affect radio-wave propagation on the Earth?

A. 28 days
B. Several hours depending on the position of the Earth in its orbit
C. Approximately 8 minutes
D. 20 to 40 hours after the radiation reaches the Earth

C Ultraviolet and X-ray radiation from the Sun travels at the speed of light, reaching the Earth in about eight minutes. (See also the discussion for questions G3A01 and G3A02.)

G3A04 What is measured by the solar flux index?

A. The density of the sun's magnetic field
B. The radio energy emitted by the sun
C. The number of sunspots on the side of the sun facing the Earth
D. A measure of the tilt of the Earth's ionosphere on the side toward the sun

B Solar flux is the radio energy coming from the Sun. High levels of solar energy produce greater ionization in the ionosphere. The solar flux measurement is taken daily by measuring radio energy from the Sun at 2800 MHz. The measurement is then converted into the solar flux index. Higher values of the solar flux index correspond to higher values of solar flux. The solar-flux measurement may be taken under any weather conditions — the Sun does not have to be visible, as it does for determining the sunspot number.

G3A05 What is the solar-flux index?

A. A measure of the highest frequency that is useful for ionospheric propagation between two points on the Earth
B. A count of sunspots which is adjusted for solar emissions
C. Another name for the American sunspot number
D. A measure of solar activity at 10.7 cm

D The solar flux index (SFI) is based on the measurement of 2800 MHz (10.7 cm wavelength) radio energy coming from the Sun. The radio energy measurement is converted to an open-ended numeric index with a minimum value of 65 (for the minimum amount of energy). Higher values of the solar flux index indicate higher levels of solar activity. (See also the discussion for question G3A04.)

G3A06   **What is a geomagnetic disturbance?**

    A. A sudden drop in the solar-flux index

    B. A shifting of the Earth's magnetic pole

    C. Ripples in the ionosphere

    D. A significant change in the Earth's magnetic field over a short period of time

D   Geomagnetic disturbances result when charged particles from a solar flare reach the Earth. When these charged particles reach the Earth's magnetic field, they are deflected toward the North and South poles. Radio communication along higher-latitude paths (latitudes greater than about 45 degrees) will be more affected than paths closer to the equator. The charged particles from the Sun may make the F-region seem to disappear or seem to split into many layers, degrading or completely blacking out long-distance radio communication.

G3A07   **Which latitudes have propagation paths that are more sensitive to geomagnetic disturbances?**

    A. Those greater than 45 degrees North or South latitude

    B. Those between 5 and 45 degrees North or South latitude

    C. Those at or very near to the equator

    D. All paths are affected equally

A   (See also the discussion for question G3A06.) Charged particles from a solar flare are directed toward the North and South magnetic poles by the Earth's magnetic field. As they enter the Earth's ionosphere, they disrupt its normal layered structure. Because the charged particles enter the ionosphere at high latitudes, radio communication paths through those regions are the most sensitive to the effects of the disruption.

G3A08   **What can be an effect of a geomagnetic storm on radio-wave propagation?**

    A. Improved high-latitude HF propagation

    B. Degraded high-latitude HF propagation

    C. Improved ground-wave propagation

    D. Improved chances of UHF ducting

B   (See the discussion for questions G3A06 and G3A07.)

G3A09 What is the effect on radio communications when sunspot numbers are high?

A. High-frequency radio signals become weak and distorted
B. Frequencies above 300 MHz become usable for long-distance communication
C. Long-distance communication in the upper HF and lower VHF range is enhanced
D. Long-distance communication in the upper HF and lower VHF range is diminished

C When sunspot numbers are high, there is a significant amount of solar activity and there will be more ionization of the ionosphere. The more the ionosphere is ionized, the higher the frequency of radio signals that may be used for long-distance communication. During the peak of a sunspot cycle, the 20 meter (14 MHz) band will be open around the world even through the night. During an unusually good sunspot cycle, even the 6 meter (50 MHz) band can become usable for long-distance communication.

G3A10 What is the sunspot number?

A. A measure of solar activity based on counting sunspots and sunspot groups
B. A 3 digit identifier which is used to track individual sunspots
C. A measure of the radio flux from the sun measured at 10.7 cm
D. A measure of the sunspot count based on radio flux measurements

A A number of observatories around the world measure solar activity. A weighted average of this data is used to determine the International Sunspot Number (ISN) for each day. These daily sunspot counts are used to produce monthly and yearly average values. The average values are used to see trends and patterns in the measurements.

Figure G3-2 — Much more than sunspots can be seen when the Sun is viewed through selective optical filters. This photo was taken through a hydrogen-alpha filter, which passes a narrow band of light wavelengths at 6562 angstroms (1 angstrom = 1×10^{-10} meters). The bright patches are active areas around and often between sunspots. Dark irregular lines are filaments of activity having no central core. Faint magnetic field lines are visible around a large central sunspot group near the disc center. *(Photo courtesy of Sacramento Peak Observatory, Sunspot, New Mexico.)*

G3A11 How long is the typical sunspot cycle?

    A. Approximately 8 minutes

    B. Between 20 and 40 hours

    C. Approximately 28 days

    D. Approximately 11 years

D The yearly averages of sunspot numbers reveal a cyclic nature of solar activity. The duration of the cycle has ranged from 9.0 to 12.7 years. The average duration is approximately 11 years. The first complete cycle to be observed systematically began in 1755, and is numbered Cycle 1. Cycle 23 began in October 1996. Solar Cycle 23 first peaked during April of 2000 with a smoothed sunspot number of 120.8. A second lower peak occurred in November of 2001 when the smoothed sunspot number was 115.6. Cycle 23 is expected to bottom out sometime during 2007 or early 2008. Cycle 24 will begin with an increase in sunspot numbers after that, so we can look forward to another peak sometime around 2011 to 2013.

G3A12 What is the K-index?

    A. An index of the relative position of sunspots on the surface of the sun

    B. A measure of the short term stability of the Earth's magnetic field

    C. A measure of the stability of the sun's magnetic field

    D. An index of solar radio flux measured at Boulder, Colorado

B The K-index represents readings of the Earth's geomagnetic field, updated every three hours at Boulder, Colorado. K-index values indicate the stability of the Earth's geomagnetic field. Steady values indicate a stable geomagnetic field, while rising values indicate an active geomagnetic field. The K-index trends are important indicators of changing propagation conditions. Rising K-index values are generally bad news for HF propagation, especially for propagation paths involving latitudes above 30° north. K-index values of 4 and rising warn of conditions associated with auroras and degraded HF propagation.

G3A13 What is the A-index?

    A. An index of the relative position of sunspots on the surface of the sun

    B. The amount of polarization of the sun's electric field

    C. An indicator of the long term stability of the Earth's geomagnetic field

    D. An index of solar radio flux measured at Boulder, Colorado

C The A-index is a daily figure for the state of activity of the Earth's magnetic field. The A-index tells you mainly about yesterday's conditions, but it is very revealing when charted regularly, because geomagnetic disturbances nearly always recur at four-week intervals. (It takes the Sun 28 days to rotate once on its axis.)

G3A14 **How are radio communications usually affected by the charged particles that reach the Earth from solar coronal holes?**

A. HF communications are improved
B. HF communications are disturbed
C. VHF/UHF ducting is improved
D. VHF/UHF ducting is disturbed

B   The corona is the Sun's outer layer. Temperatures in the corona are typically about two million degrees Celsius, but can be more than four million degrees Celsius over an active sunspot region. A coronal hole is an area of somewhat lower temperature. Matter ejected through such a "hole" is in the form of plasma, a highly ionized gas made up of electrons, protons and neutral particles. The plasma travels at speeds up to two million miles per hour, and if the "jet" of material is directed toward the Earth it can result in a geomagnetic storm on Earth, disrupting HF communication.

G3A15 **How long does it take charged particles from Coronal Mass Ejections to affect radio-wave propagation on the Earth?**

A. 28 days
B. 14 days
C. The effect is instantaneous
D. 20 to 40 hours

D   (See also the discussion for question G3A14.) Matter ejected from the corona is a plasma made up of electrons, protons, ions and neutral particles. The plasma travels at speeds of two million miles per hour or more, so it can take about 20 to 40 hours for the plasma to travel the 93 million miles to Earth.

G3A16 **What is a possible benefit to radio communications resulting from periods of high geomagnetic activity?**

A. Aurora that can reflect VHF signals
B. Higher signal strength for HF signals passing through the polar regions
C. Improved HF long path propagation
D. Reduced long delayed echoes

A   When the plasma, or charged particles, from a coronal mass ejection reaches the Earth it interacts with the Earth's magnetic field. The charged particles follow magnetic field lines into the Earth's atmosphere near the North and South magnetic poles, producing visible aurora borealis at northern latitudes and aurora australis in the south. VHF operators look forward to such conditions because radio signals can be reflected from auroral "patches," making long-distance contacts possible.

G3A17 At what point in the solar cycle does the 20 meter band usually support worldwide propagation during daylight hours?

A. At the summer solstice
B. Only at the maximum point of the solar cycle
C. Only at the minimum point of the solar cycle
D. At any point in the solar cycle

D Even at the minimum point of the solar cycle, worldwide propagation is possible on the 20 meter band. As solar activity increases, the band will remain open for longer periods and with stronger signal strengths. For this reason, 20 meters is a favorite band for "DXers."

G3A18 If the HF radio-wave propagation (skip) is generally good on the 24-MHz and 28-MHz bands for several days, when might you expect a similar condition to occur?

A. 7 days later
B. 14 days later
C. 28 days later
D. 90 days later

C It takes approximately 28 days for the Sun to rotate on its axis. Since active areas on the Sun may persist for four or five months, you can expect good propagation conditions to recur approximately every 28 days for four or five months.

G3A19 Which frequencies are least reliable for long distance communications during periods of low solar activity?

A. Frequencies below 3.5 MHz
B. Frequencies near 3.5 MHz
C. Frequencies at or above 10 MHz
D. Frequencies above 20 MHz

D The higher the frequency, the more ionization is needed in the ionosphere to refract (bend) the radio signal back to the Earth. When solar activity is low, the higher frequencies will pass through the ionosphere into space instead of being refracted back to Earth. During periods of low solar activity, the 15 meter (21 MHz), 12 meter (24.9 MHz) and 10 meter (28 MHz) bands are the least reliable HF bands for long distance communication.

G3B   Maximum Usable Frequency; Lowest Usable Frequency; propagation "hops"

G3B01   Which band should offer the best chance for a successful contact if the maximum usable frequency (MUF) between the two stations is 22 MHz?

A. 10 meters
B. 15 meters
C. 20 meters
D. 40 meters

B   The best long-distance propagation will be found on frequencies just below the MUF. The highest frequencies amateurs may use below 22 MHz are on the 15 meter (21 MHz) band. (See also the discussion for question G3B05.)

G3B02   Which band should offer the best chance for a successful contact if the maximum usable frequency (MUF) between the two stations is 16 MHz?

A. 80 meters
B. 40 meters
C. 20 meters
D. 2 meters

C   The best long-distance propagation will be found on frequencies just below the MUF. The highest frequencies amateurs may use below 16 MHz are on the 20 meter (14 MHz) band. (See also the discussion for question G3B05.)

G3B03   Which of the following guidelines should be selected for lowest attenuation when transmitting on HF?

A. Select a frequency just below the MUF
B. Select a frequency just above the LUF
C. Select a frequency just below the critical frequency
D. Select a frequency just above the critical frequency

A   Ionospheric absorption (attenuation) is lowest just below the Maximum Usable Frequency (MUF). Use a frequency just below the MUF for the highest received signal strength. (See also the discussion for question G3B05.)

G3B04 What is a reliable way to determine if the maximum usable frequency (MUF) is high enough to support 28-MHz propagation between your station and Western Europe?

A. Listen for signals on a 28 MHz international beacon
B. Send a series of dots on the 28 MHz band and listen for echoes from your signal
C. Check the strength of TV signals from Western Europe
D. Listen to WWV propagation signals on the 28 MHz band

A Beacon stations transmit signals so that amateur operators can evaluate propagation conditions. By listening for beacon stations from Western Europe, you will be able to determine if the MUF is high enough for 10-meter communication to that area. (See also the discussion for question G3B05.)

G3B05 What usually happens to radio waves with frequencies below the maximum usable frequency (MUF) when they are sent into the ionosphere?

A. They are bent back to the Earth
B. They pass through the ionosphere
C. They are completely absorbed by the ionosphere
D. They are bent and trapped in the ionosphere to circle the Earth

A The maximum usable frequency (MUF) relates to a particular desired destination. The MUF is the highest frequency that will allow the radio wave to reach its desired destination using E- or F-region propagation. There is no single MUF for a given transmitter location; it will vary depending on the direction and distance to the station you are attempting to contact. Signals with frequencies lower than the MUF are generally bent back to Earth. Signals with frequencies higher than the MUF will pass through the ionosphere instead of being bent back to the Earth.

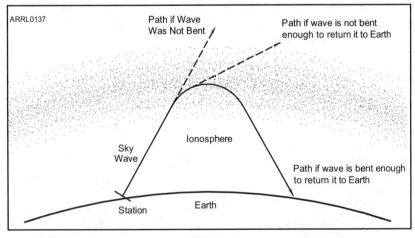

Figure G3-3 — Radio waves are bent in the ionosphere, so they return to Earth far from the transmitter. If the radio wave is not bent (refracted) enough in the ionosphere, it will pass into space rather than returning to Earth.

G3B06 What usually happens to radio waves with frequencies below the lowest usable frequency (LUF)?

A. They are bent back to the Earth
B. They pass through the ionosphere
C. They are completely absorbed by the ionosphere
D. They are bent and trapped in the ionosphere to circle the Earth

C The lowest usable frequency (LUF) is the frequency at which ionospheric absorption attenuates the radio signals to below the atmospheric noise levels. Since absorption increases with decreasing frequency, signals at frequencies below the LUF cannot be received via sky-wave communication.

G3B07 What does LUF stand for?

A. The Lowest Usable Frequency for communications between two points
B. The Longest Universal Function for communications between two points
C. The Lowest Usable Frequency during a 24 hour period
D. The Longest Universal Function during a 24 hour period

A See the discussion for question G3B06.

G3B08 What does MUF stand for?

A. The Minimum Usable Frequency for communications between two points
B. The Maximum Usable Frequency for communications between two points
C. The Minimum Usable Frequency during a 24 hour period
D. The Maximum Usable Frequency during a 24 hour period

B See the discussion for question G3B05.

G3B09   What is the maximum distance along the Earth's surface that is normally covered in one hop using the F2 region?

- A. 180 miles
- B. 1,200 miles
- C. 2,500 miles
- D. 12,000 miles

C   The F region forms and decays in correlation with the daily passage of the Sun. The F1 and F2 regions form when the F region splits into two parts when receiving high radiation from the Sun, recombining into a single F region at night. The more solar radiation the F region receives, the more it is ionized so it reaches maximum ionization shortly after noon during the summertime. The ionization tapers off very gradually toward sunset and the F2 region remains usable into the night. The F2 region is the highest region of the ionosphere, reaching as high as 300 miles at noon in the summertime. Because the F2 region is the highest ionospheric region, it is the region mainly responsible for long-distance communication. A one-hop transmission can travel a maximum distance of about 2500 miles using this F2 region.

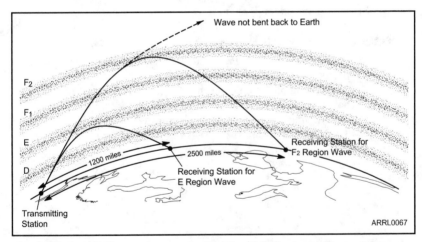

Figure G3-4 — Radio waves are refracted (bent) in the ionosphere and may return to Earth. If the radio waves are refracted to Earth from the F2 region, they may return to Earth about 2500 miles from the transmitting station. If the radio waves are refracted to Earth from the E region, they may return to Earth about 1200 miles from the transmitting station.

G3B10 **What is the maximum distance along the Earth's surface that is normally covered in one hop using the E region?**

A. 180 miles
B. 1,200 miles
C. 2,500 miles
D. 12,000 miles

B The E region of the ionosphere is the second lowest (above the D region). The E region appears at an altitude of about 70 miles above the Earth. The E region ionizes during the daytime, but the ionization does not last very long after sunset. Ionization of the E region is at a maximum around midday. During the daytime, a radio signal can travel a maximum distance of about 1200 miles in one hop using the E region.

G3B11 **What happens to HF propagation when the lowest usable frequency (LUF) exceeds the maximum usable frequency (MUF)?**

A. No HF radio frequency will support communications over the path
B. HF communications over the path are enhanced at the frequency where the LUF and MUF are the same
C. Double hop propagation along the path is more common
D. Propagation over the path on all HF frequencies is enhanced

A Signals at frequencies below the lowest usable frequency (LUF) will be absorbed in the ionosphere rather than returning to Earth. Occasionally the LUF may be higher than the maximum usable frequency (MUF). This means that for the highest possible frequency that will propagate through the ionosphere for that path, the signal absorption is so large that even signals at the MUF are absorbed. Under these conditions it is impossible to establish sky-wave communication between those two points no matter what frequency is used! (Communication between either location and other locations may be possible, though, because the LUF and MUF depend on the end points of the communication path.)

G3B12   What factors affect the maximum usable frequency (MUF)?

A. Path distance and location
B. Time of day and season
C. Solar radiation and ionospheric disturbance
D. All of these choices are correct

D   Maximum usable frequency (MUF) refers to the highest frequency that will provide sky-wave propagation between two specific locations. For example, suppose you live in Illinois and want to communicate with another amateur in Ecuador. You might find that the MUF for this contact is about 18 MHz at 1400 UTC. You may also find that the MUF to communicate with a station in Spain at that same time is 12 MHz. Different communication path distances and directions will often result in very different MUF values. The MUF depends on conditions in the ionosphere, and those conditions will vary by time of day as well as the season of the year. The amount of solar radiation striking the ionosphere varies significantly depending on the timing of the 11-year sunspot cycle. Any solar flares, coronal-mass ejections and other disturbances on the Sun can also result in ionospheric disturbances that will affect the MUF. Answer choices A, B and C all describe factors that will affect the MUF for a given sky-wave propagation path, so answer choice D is correct.

G3B13   How might a sky-wave signal sound if it arrives at your receiver by both short path and long path propagation?

A. Periodic fading approximately every 10 seconds
B. Signal strength increased by 3 dB
C. The signal will be cancelled causing severe attenuation
D. A well-defined echo can be heard

D   Normally, you will expect radio signals to arrive at your station by following the shortest possible path between you and the transmitting station. This is called short-path propagation. Signals that might have arrived from the opposite direction, 180 degrees different from the short-path signals, are normally so weak that you would probably not hear them. Signals that arrive 180 degrees from the short path are called long-path signals. When propagation conditions are suitable, the long-path signals may be strong enough to support communication. In fact, there are times when the long-path propagation may be even better than the short-path propagation. Stations with directional antennas can point their antennas directly away from each other to communicate. (This is not simply communicating using signals radiated "off the back" of the antennas.) If you are listening to signals on your receiver and you hear a well-defined echo, even if it is a weak echo, the chances are you are hearing signals arrive at your station over the long path. The slightly longer time it takes the signals to travel the longer distance around the Earth results in a slight delay when compared to the direct, short-path signals. This is a good indication that you may be able to point your antenna directly away from the received station to communicate.

G3B14 **Which of the following is a good indicator of the possibility of sky-wave propagation on the 6 meter band?**

A. Short hop sky-wave propagation on the 10 meter band
B. Long hop sky-wave propagation on the 10 meter band
C. Severe attenuation of signals on the 10 meter band
D. Long delayed echoes on the 10 meter band

A As the maximum usable frequency (MUF) for a given path increases, the ionosphere also supports shorter single-hop distance at lower frequencies. Suppose you are operating on the 10-meter band, and are contacting stations that are 800 to 1000 miles away. After making a few more contacts you start to notice that you are contacting stations only about 500 miles away, and then you notice that you are contacting stations even closer, perhaps only out to a few hundred miles. This can be an excellent indication that the MUF for the longer-path stations has moved up to a higher frequency, perhaps even above 50 MHz. It is a good time to check for a band opening on 6 meters!

G3C Ionospheric layers; critical angle and frequency; HF scatter; Near Vertical Incidence Sky waves

G3C01 Which of the following ionospheric layers is closest to the surface of the Earth?

A. The D layer
B. The E layer
C. The F1 layer
D. The F2 layer

A The D region of the ionosphere is the lowest, forming at a height of 30 to 60 miles. Because it is the lowest, it is also the densest and its ionization disappears by dark.

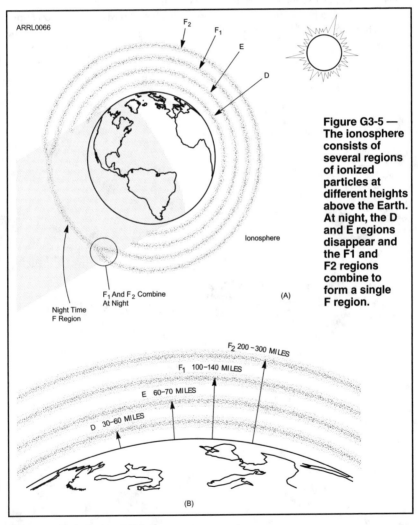

ARRL0066

Ionosphere

F_1 And F_2 Combine At Night

(A)

Night Time F Region

Figure G3-5 — The ionosphere consists of several regions of ionized particles at different heights above the Earth. At night, the D and E regions disappear and the F1 and F2 regions combine to form a single F region.

F_2 200~300 MILES

F_1 100-140 MILES

E 60-70 MILES

D 30-60 MILES

(B)

G3C02 **When can the F2 region be expected to reach its maximum height at your location?**

A. At noon during the summer
B. At midnight during the summer
C. At dusk in the spring and fall
D. At noon during the winter

A The F region forms and decays in correlation with the daily passage of the Sun. The F1 and F2 regions form when the F region splits into two parts when receiving high radiation from the Sun, recombining into a single F region at night. The more solar radiation the F region receives, the more it is ionized so it reaches maximum ionization shortly after noon during the summertime. The ionization tapers off very gradually toward sunset and the F2 region remains usable into the night. The F2 region is the highest region of the ionosphere, reaching as high as 300 miles at noon in the summertime.

G3C03 **Why is the F2 region mainly responsible for the longest distance radio wave propagation?**

A. Because it is the densest ionospheric layer
B. Because it does not absorb radio waves as much as other ionospheric regions
C. Because it is the highest ionospheric region
D. All of these choices are correct

C (See also the discussion for question G3B09.) Because the F2 region is the highest ionospheric region, it is the region mainly responsible for long-distance communication. A one-hop transmission can travel a maximum distance of about 2500 miles using this F2 region.

G3C04 **What does the term "critical angle" mean as used in radio wave propagation?**

A. The long path azimuth of a distant station
B. The short path azimuth of a distant station
C. The lowest takeoff angle that will return a radio wave to the Earth under specific ionospheric conditions
D. The highest takeoff angle that will return a radio wave to the Earth under specific ionospheric conditions

D At each frequency there is a maximum angle for which the radio wave can leave the antenna and still be refracted back to Earth by the ionosphere instead of simply passing through it and proceeding out into space. The critical angle changes depending on the ionization of the ionosphere.

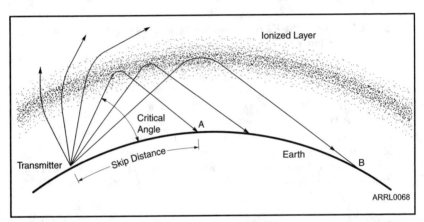

Figure G3-6 — Radio waves that leave the transmitting antenna at an angle higher than the critical angle are not refracted enough to return to Earth. A radio wave at the critical angle will return to Earth. The lowest-angle wave will return to Earth farther away than the wave at the critical angle. This illustrates the importance of low radiation angles for working DX.

G3C05 Why is long distance communication on the 40, 60, 80 and
160 meter bands more difficult during the day?

A. The F layer absorbs these frequencies during daylight hours
B. The F layer is unstable during daylight hours
C. The D layer absorbs these frequencies during daylight hours
D. The E layer is unstable during the daylight hours

C   Think of the D region as the Darned Daylight region. The D region does not
bend high frequency signals back to Earth. What it does instead is absorb energy
from radio waves. Signals at lower frequencies (longer wavelengths such as 160,
80, 60 and 40 meters) are absorbed more than at higher frequencies. The ionization
created by the sunlight does not last very long in the D region, disappearing by
sunset.

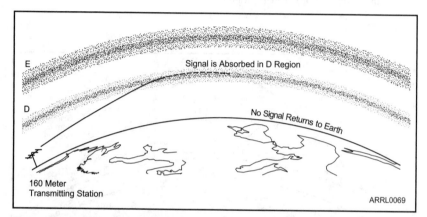

**Figure G3-7 — The D region of the ionosphere absorbs energy from radio
waves. Lower-frequency radio waves don't make it all the way through the D
region, so the waves do not return to Earth. Higher-frequency waves travel
through the D region, and are then refracted (bent) back to Earth.**

G3C06 **What is a characteristic of HF scatter signals?**

    A. They have high intelligibility
    B. They have a wavering sound
    C. They have very large swings in signal strength
    D. All of these choices are correct

B   The area between the farthest reach of ground-wave propagation and the point where signals are refracted back from the ionosphere (sky-wave propagation) is called the skip zone. Since some of the transmitted signal is scattered in the atmosphere or from ground reflections, communication may be possible in the skip zone by the use of scatter signals. The amount of signal scattered in the atmosphere will be quite small and the signal received in the skip zone will arrive from several radio-wave paths. This tends to produce a weak, distorted signal with a fluttering or wavering sound.

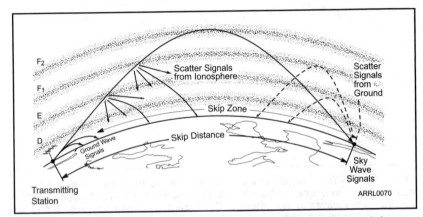

Figure G3-8 — Radio waves may be reflected back toward the transmitting station from variations in the ionosphere or after striking the ground after ionospheric reflection. Some of this energy may be scattered back into the skip zone as a weak, highly variable signal.

G3C07 **What makes HF scatter signals often sound distorted?**

    A. The ionospheric layer involved is unstable
    B. Ground waves are absorbing much of the signal
    C. The E-region is not present
    D. Energy is scattered into the skip zone through several radio wave paths

D   The amount of signal scattered back toward the transmitting station from the ionosphere or ground will be quite small. The signal received in the skip zone will also arrive from several radio-wave paths. This tends to produce a weak, distorted signal with a fluttering or wavering sound. (See also the discussion for question G3C06.)

G3C08 Why are HF scatter signals in the skip zone usually weak?

A. Only a small part of the signal energy is scattered into the skip zone
B. Signals are scattered from the troposphere which is not a good reflector
C. Propagation is through ground waves which absorb most of the signal energy
D. Propagation is through ducts in F region which absorb most of the energy

A   The amount of signal scattered back toward the transmitting station from the ionosphere or ground will be quite small. The signal received in the skip zone will also arrive from several radio-wave paths. This tends to produce a weak, distorted signal with a fluttering or wavering sound. (See also the discussion for question G3C06.)

G3C09 What type of radio wave propagation allows a signal to be detected at a distance too far for ground wave propagation but too near for normal sky wave propagation?

A. Ground wave
B. Scatter
C. Sporadic-E skip
D. Short-path skip

B   The area between the farthest reach of ground-wave propagation and the point where signals are refracted back from the ionosphere (sky-wave propagation) is called the skip zone. Since some of the transmitted signal is scattered in the atmosphere, communication may be possible in the skip zone by the use of scatter signals. (See also the discussion for question G3C06.)

G3C10 Which of the following might be an indication that signals heard on the HF bands are being received via scatter propagation?

A. The communication is during a sunspot maximum
B. The communication is during a sudden ionospheric disturbance
C. The signal is heard on a frequency below the maximum usable frequency
D. The signal is heard on a frequency above the maximum usable frequency

D   Frequencies above the maximum usable frequency (MUF) normally pass through the ionosphere out into space rather than being bent back, although atmospheric scatter from the ionosphere will sometimes allow communication on these frequencies. Amateurs trying to communicate on frequencies that seem to be above the MUF may notice that they can communicate using these scattered signals. Had they been using a frequency below the MUF they may not have noticed any scattered signals. (See also the discussion for question G3C06.)

G3C11 **Which of the following is true about ionospheric absorption near the maximum usable frequency (MUF)?**

A. Absorption will be minimum

B. Absorption is greater for vertically polarized waves

C. Absorption approaches maximum

D. Absorption is greater for horizontally polarized waves

A As a general rule, less of your signal will be absorbed by the ionosphere if you are using a frequency close to the maximum usable frequency (MUF). (See also the discussion for question G3B05.)

G3C12 **Which ionospheric layer is the most absorbent of long skip signals during daylight hours on frequencies below 10 MHz?**

A. The F2 layer

B. The F1 layer

C. The E layer

D. The D layer

D See the discussion for question G3C05.

G3C13 What is Near Vertical Incidence Sky-wave (NVIS) propagation?

A. Propagation near the MUF
B. Short distance HF propagation using high elevation angles
C. Long path HF propagation at sunrise and sunset
D. Double hop propagation near the LUF

B Near Vertical Incidence Sky-wave (NVIS) propagation refers to communication using sky-wave signals transmitted at very high vertical angles. The frequencies used are below the critical frequency, meaning that their critical angle (see question G3C04) is ninety degrees, meaning they can be reflected straight back down to Earth. Because the signals travel at high angles, they spend little time passing through and so encounter a minimum amount of attenuation from the D and E layers. The result is good communication in a region around the transmitter over distances higher than supported by ground-wave propagation.

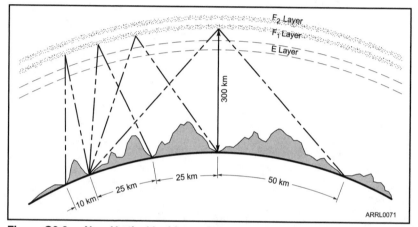

Figure G3-9 — Near Vertical Incidence Sky-wave (NVIS) communication relies on signals below the critical frequency transmitted at high vertical angles. The signals are reflected by the ionosphere back to Earth in the region around the transmitter.

G3C14 Which of the following antennas will be most effective for skip communications on 40 meters during the day?

A. A vertical antenna
B. A horizontal dipole placed between 1/8 and 1/4 wavelength above the ground
C. A left-hand circularly polarized antenna
D. A right-hand circularly polarized antenna

B Low horizontal antennas, such as dipoles between 1/8 and 1/4 wavelength above the ground, work best for daytime skip communication on low frequencies. Signals from such antennas are radiated at high vertical angles that can be reflected by the ionosphere, but the signals have a minimum amount of attenuation from the D and E layers.

Amateur Radio Practices

Your General class exam (Element 3) will consist of 35 questions taken from the General class question pool as prepared by the Volunteer Examiner Coordinators' Question Pool Committee. A certain number of questions are taken from each of the 10 subelements. There will be 5 questions from the subelement shown in this chapter. These questions are divided into 5 groups, labeled G4A through G4E.

G4A Two-tone Test; amplifier tuning and neutralization; DSP

G4A01 Which of the following is one use for a DSP in an amateur station?

A. To provide adequate grounding
B. To remove noise from received signals
C. To increase antenna gain
D. To increase antenna bandwidth

B Digital Signal Processing (DSP) is the process of converting analog signals to digital data, processing them with software programs, then converting the signals back to analog form. Digital noise reduction is but one application — filtering, demodulation and decoding are also commonly performed by DSP circuits.

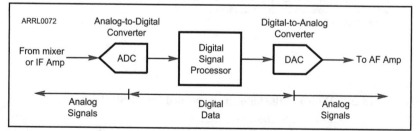

Figure G4-1 — A DSP circuit consists of an analog-to-digital converter (ADC), a microprocessor that operates on the digitized data, and a digital-to-analog converter (DAC) that converts the signal back to analog.

G4A02 **Which of the following instruments may be used to measure the output of a single-sideband transmitter when performing a two-tone test of amplitude linearity?**

A. An audio distortion analyzer
B. An oscilloscope
C. A directional wattmeter
D. A high impedance audio voltmeter

B   It is common to test the amplitude linearity of a single-sideband transmitter by injecting two audio tones of equal level into the microphone jack, then observing the pattern made on an oscilloscope. To get meaningful results, the two tones must not be harmonically related to each other (such as 1 and 2 kHz). Of course the audio tones must be within the audio passband of the transmitter to display on the oscilloscope. The ARRL Lab uses 700 Hz and 1900 Hz tones to perform this test.

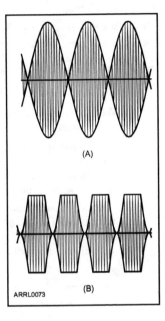

(A)

(B)

ARRL0073

Figure G4-2 — The two-tone test waveform at A is from a properly operating SSB transmitter. Note the smooth sine-wave shape of the curves, especially as they cross the zero axis. The two-tone test waveform at B is from a transmitter that has severe flat-topping and crossover distortion. Notice the different shape of the waveform where it crosses the zero-amplitude horizontal axis, as compared to the waveform shown at A.

G4A03 **Which of the following is needed for a DSP IF filter?**

A. An Analog to Digital Converter
B. Digital to Analog Converter
C. A Digital Processor Chip
D. All of the these answers are correct

D   See the discussion for question G4A01.

G4A04 **Which of the following is an advantage of a receiver IF filter created with a DSP as compared to an analog filter?**

A. A wide range of filter bandwidths and shapes can be created
B. Fewer digital components are required
C. Mixing products are greatly reduced
D. The DSP filter is much more effective at VHF frequencies

A DSP circuits use software to process the digitized signal, so the number of different functions that can be performed is limited only by the amount of memory to contain program instructions. In addition, unlike most analog filters, parameters such as bandwidth and the shape of the response can be made adjustable by the operator. This provides a great deal of flexibility in receiver operation.

G4A05 **How is DSP filtering accomplished?**

A. By using direct signal phasing
B. By converting the signal from analog to digital and using digital processing
C. By up-converting the signal to VHF
D. By converting the signal from digital to analog and taking the difference of mixing products

B See the discussion for question G4A01.

G4A06 **What reading on the plate current meter of a vacuum tube RF power amplifier indicates correct adjustment of the plate tuning control?**

A. A pronounced peak
B. A pronounced dip
C. No change will be observed
D. A slow, rhythmic oscillation

B The plate tuning control of a vacuum tube RF amplifier — either of a standalone amplifier or of a transmitter output stage — adjusts the impedance matching circuit for the proper frequency of operation. When that frequency is reached, plate current is minimized for a particular level of power output. As the control is adjusted, the pronounced "dip" in plate current indicates when the tuning control is properly adjusted. The Load or Coupling control is then used to adjust the amount of output power. The tuning and load controls are successively adjusted until the required amount of output power is obtained without exceeding the tube's plate current rating.

G4A07 What is the correct adjustment for the "Load" or "Coupling" control of a vacuum tube RF power amplifier?

A. Minimum SWR on the antenna
B. Minimum plate current without exceeding maximum allowable grid current
C. Highest plate voltage while minimizing grid current
D. Maximum power output without exceeding maximum allowable plate current

D See the discussion for question G4A06.

G4A08 Which of the following techniques is used to neutralize an RF amplifier?

A. Feed-forward compensation
B. Feed-forward cancellation
C. Negative feedback
D. Positive feedback

C Neutralization of a power amplifier is a technique designed to minimize or cancel the effects of positive feedback. Positive feedback occurs when the output signal is fed back to the input in phase with the input signal. As a result, the amplifier may self-oscillate. You can demonstrate this principle by observing the squeal that occurs when you hold a microphone in front of a speaker. Neutralization consists of feeding a portion of the amplifier output back to the input, 180 degrees out of phase with the input, to cancel the positive feedback. This is called negative feedback.

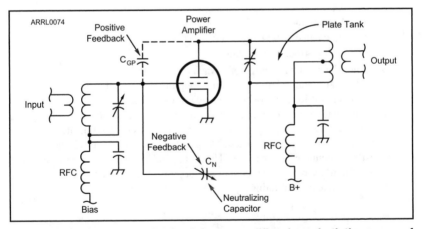

Figure G4-3 — The schematic circuit for an amplifier shows both the source of positive feedback that can create self-oscillation and negative feedback that cancels or neutralizes the positive feedback. Positive feedback is created by the capacitance from the plate to the grid, shows as C_{GP} on the schematic. The amount of capacitance is small, so the frequency of self-oscillation is usually at VHF or in the upper HF range. Capacitor C_N is connected to a point in the output circuit at which the signal has the opposite phase, so the feedback to the grid acts as negative feedback by providing an equal-and-opposite feedback signal to that from C_{GP}.

G4A09 What does a neutralizing circuit do in an RF amplifier?

    A. It controls differential gain

    B. It cancels the effects of positive feedback

    C. It eliminates AC hum from the power supply

    D. It reduces incidental grid modulation

B   See the discussion for question G4A08.

G4A10 What is the reason for neutralizing the final amplifier stage of a transmitter?

    A. To limit the modulation index

    B. To eliminate self oscillations

    C. To cut off the final amplifier during standby periods

    D. To keep the carrier on frequency

B   Neutralization prevents the amplifier from self-oscillating. Self-oscillation creates powerful spurious signals that cause interference. Self-oscillations can also be sufficiently powerful to damage the amplifier.

G4A11 What type of transmitter performance does a two-tone test analyze?

    A. Linearity

    B. Carrier and undesired sideband suppression

    C. Percentage of frequency modulation

    D. Percentage of carrier phase shift

A   A two-tone test checks the linearity of a single-sideband transmitter. (See also the discussion for question G4A02.)

G4A12 What type of signals are used to conduct a two-tone test?

    A. Two audio signals of the same frequency shifted 90-degrees

    B. Two non-harmonically related audio signals

    C. Two swept frequency tones

    D. Two audio frequency range square wave signals of equal amplitude

B   The two audio tones must be within the audio passband of the transmitter and not be harmonically related to each other (such as 1000 and 2000 Hz, the second harmonic of 1000 Hz). The ARRL Lab uses 700 Hz and 1900 Hz tones to perform this test.

G4A13 **Which of the following performs automatic notching of interfering carriers?**

A. Band pass tuning
B. A DSP filter
C. Balanced mixing
D. A noise limiter

B The software program that controls a DSP notch filter may also operate automatically. In this type of operation, the software searches for the steady tones of an interfering carrier, such as from a shortwave broadcast signal, and then adjusts the frequency of the notch until the amplitude of the carrier's tone is minimized. (See also the discussion for question G4A01.)

G4B Test and monitoring equipment

G4B01 **What item of test equipment contains horizontal and vertical channel amplifiers?**

A. An ohmmeter
B. A signal generator
C. An ammeter
D. An oscilloscope

D An oscilloscope uses one signal to deflect a beam of electrons horizontally across the face of the screen and a second signal to deflect the beam vertically. The electron beam causes a phosphor coating on the inside of the screen to glow so that the beam's position can be observed. The horizontal and vertical channel amplifiers in the oscilloscope increase the voltage of the two input signals for the desired amount of deflection. Most oscilloscopes have a built-in oscillator circuit, called a sweep generator, designed to repeatedly deflect the electron beam horizontally across the screen at a fixed rate. With an external signal applied to the vertical amplifier, the sweep generator frequency is adjusted to produce a stable pattern on the screen. Some oscilloscopes also allow a second input signal to be applied to a separate horizontal channel amplifier. This allows two signals to be compared to each other with respect to time.

G4B02 **Which of the following is an advantage of an oscilloscope versus a digital voltmeter?**

A. An oscilloscope uses less power
B. Complex impedances can be easily measured
C. Input impedance is much lower
D. Complex waveforms can be measured

D Digital voltmeters display measured values of voltage with excellent precision but they can not measure a complex signal waveform's time-related parameters, such as its frequency or period, or how it reacts to other signals.

G4B03 How would a signal tracer normally be used?

A. To identify the source of radio transmissions
B. To make exact drawings of signal waveforms
C. To show standing wave patterns on open-wire feed-lines
D. To identify an inoperative stage in a receiver

D   A signal tracer is any device that reacts to RF or AF energy and is used to trace the path of a signal through a circuit. A signal tracer can help identify an inoperative stage in a receiver. Some signal tracers also include signal sources to inject signals into receiver stages for testing.

G4B04 How is a noise bridge normally used?

A. It is connected at an antenna's feed point and reads the antenna's noise figure
B. It is connected between a transmitter and an antenna and tuned for minimum SWR
C. It is connected between a receiver and an antenna of unknown impedance and is adjusted for minimum noise
D. It is connected between an antenna and ground and tuned for minimum SWR

C   A noise bridge is a device that applies a wideband noise signal to a circuit to measure the circuit impedance. A receiver tuned to the desired frequency is also placed in the circuit. Adjust the noise bridge to minimize the noise received, and then observe the readings on the noise bridge controls. The settings of the noise bridge controls indicate the circuit impedance.

G4B05 Which of the following is the better instrument to use to check the keying waveform of a CW transmitter?

A. A monitoring oscilloscope
B. A field-strength meter
C. A sidetone monitor
D. A wavemeter

A   An oscilloscope visually displays a signal waveform. This allows you to observe the shape of the CW signal (referred to as the CW envelope) noting, for example, the rise and fall time of the signal. It also allows you to observe problems such as flat-topping (caused by overmodulation) on your SSB signal.

G4B06 What signal source is connected to the vertical input of a monitoring oscilloscope when checking the quality of a transmitted signal?

A. The local oscillator of the transmitter
B. The audio input of the transmitter
C. The transmitter balanced mixer output
D. The attenuated RF output of the transmitter

D When the RF output from a transmitter is connected to the vertical channel of an oscilloscope, the oscilloscope visually displays the signal's envelope. This allows you to check for signal distortion such as flat-topping (caused by overmodulation).

G4B07 What is an advantage of a digital voltmeter as compared to an analog voltmeter?

A. Better for measuring computer circuits
B. Better for RF measurements
C. Significantly better precision for most uses
D. Faster response

C A digital voltmeter displays measurements of voltage, current and resistance in numeric form instead of using a moving needle and a fixed scale. The digital voltmeter has significantly better precision than an analog meter. Analog meters, however, may be a better choice for adjusting a circuit for peak and minimum values because the needle movement is easier to see and read than a changing numeric display.

G4B08 What instrument may be used to monitor relative RF output when making antenna and transmitter adjustments?

A. A field-strength meter
B. An antenna noise bridge
C. A multimeter
D. A Q meter

A A field-strength meter makes a relative measurement of the intensity of the field being radiated from an antenna. Some amateurs keep a field-strength meter in their shack to monitor the relative RF output from their station. This can be especially handy when you are making antenna or transmitter adjustments.

G4B09 How much must the power output of a transmitter be raised to change the "S" meter reading on a distant receiver from S8 to S9?

A. Approximately 2 times
B. Approximately 3 times
C. Approximately 4 times
D. Approximately 5 times

C A theoretical, ideal S meter operates on a logarithmic scale, indicating one S unit of change for a four-times increase or decrease in power. (This is a 6-dB change in power.) In real life, S meters are only calibrated to this standard in the middle of their range (if at all). In the example of this question, to raise the reading on an ideal S meter from S8 to S9, the transmitter power would have to be increased by a factor of 4. Increasing the transmitter power from 5 watts to 20 watts, for example would raise a received signal from S8 to S9.

G4B10 Which of the following can be determined with a field strength meter?

A. The radiation resistance of an antenna
B. The radiation pattern of an antenna
C. The presence and amount of phase distortion of a transmitter
D. The presence and amount of amplitude distortion of a transmitter

B A field-strength meter makes a relative measurement of the intensity of the field being radiated from an antenna. By placing the field-strength meter in different locations around the antenna, you can determine the relative field pattern of the antenna.

G4B11 Which of the following might be a use for a field strength meter?

A. Close-in radio direction-finding
B. A modulation monitor for a frequency or phase modulation transmitter
C. An overmodulation indicator for a SSB transmitter
D. A keying indicator for a RTTY or packet transmitter

A A field-strength meter makes a relative measurement of the intensity of the field being radiated from an antenna. If you are doing some radio direction finding (RDF), you may find that a field strength meter is a handy piece of equipment to use as you get close to the transmitter source. A strong signal may drive the S meter off scale, and this would require a variable attenuator to be used between the directional antenna and receiver as you get closer to the transmitter. A field-strength meter could replace the normal RDF equipment under those conditions, and you can use your body to shield the field-strength meter to find the direction to the transmitter.

G4B12 **What is one way a noise bridge might be used?**

A. Determining an antenna's gain in dBi
B. Pre-tuning an antenna tuner
C. Pre-tuning a linear amplifier
D. Determining the line loss of the antenna system

B   A noise bridge is a device that applies a wideband noise signal to a circuit to test the circuit impedance. A receiver on the desired frequency is also placed in the circuit. Normally, you would adjust the noise bridge to minimize the noise received, and then observe the readings on the noise bridge controls. The markings on the noise bridge controls indicate the circuit impedance. Another way to make use of a noise bridge is to set the controls for a 50-ohm resistance and zero reactance, then adjust an antenna tuner for minimum received noise. This "pre-adjusts" the antenna tuner to approximately the right settings before applying any transmitter power to the antenna tuner and antenna.

G4B13 **What is one measurement that can be made with a dip meter?**

A. The resonant frequency of a circuit
B. The tilt of the ionosphere
C. The gain of an antenna
D. The notch depth of a filter

A   A dip meter is a standalone variable-frequency oscillator with a tuned circuit whose coil is mounted externally so that it can be placed near the circuit to be tested. A meter indicates the amount of power in the oscillator's tuned circuit. When the oscillator's frequency is adjusted to the resonant frequency of the external circuit, power is coupled from the dip meter's coil to the external circuit and the meter shows a sudden drop.

G4B14 **Which of the following must be connected to an antenna analyzer when it is being used for SWR measurements?**

A. Receiver
B. Transmitter
C. Antenna and feedline
D. All of these answers are correct

C   An antenna analyzer is the equivalent of a very low power, adjustable frequency transmitter and SWR bridge. The antenna and feed line are connected to the analyzer and SWR measurements are made directly from the analyzer's meter or display while the analyzer frequency is adjusted. This is much more convenient than using a transmitter and wattmeter and also minimizes the potential for interfering with other signals.

G4B15 **Which of the following can be measured with a directional wattmeter?**

A. Standing Wave Ratio
B. Antenna front-to-back ratio
C. RF interference
D. Radio wave propagation

A Standing wave ratio (SWR) can be calculated from forward and reflected power measurements made using a directional wattmeter. SWR is then calculated using the following formula:

$$SWR = \frac{1 + \sqrt{P_R / P_F}}{1 - \sqrt{P_R / P_F}}$$

G4B16 **Why is high input impedance desirable for a voltmeter?**

A. It improves the frequency response
B. It decreases battery consumption in the meter
C. It improves the resolution of the readings
D. It decreases the loading on circuits being measured

D The higher the impedance of a voltmeter, the smaller the amount of current drawn from the circuit being tested. This allows the voltmeter to make an accurate measurement of voltage while disturbing the circuit as little as possible.

G4C01 Which of the following might be useful in reducing RF interference to audio-frequency devices?

A. Bypass inductor
B. Bypass capacitor
C. Forward-biased diode
D. Reverse-biased diode

B If radio frequency interference is entering a home audio system through external speaker wires, bypassing the wires to the chassis through capacitors at the speaker terminals is usually effective. (In practice, it's a little more complicated than this. With transistor audio amplifiers you may need to use RF chokes in series with the speaker leads, as well as bypass capacitors. See the ARRL Handbook and The ARRL RFI Book for more information on finding and fixing RFI problems.)

Figure G4-4 — This diagram shows a filter that can be used at the output of some transistor audio amplifiers. The capacitors bypass the undesired signals to ground. C1 and C2 are 0.001 to 0.05-μF disc ceramic, 1.4-kV capacitors. RFC1 and RFC2 are 24 turns of number 18 AWG enameled wire, close spaced and wound on a ¼ inch diameter form (such as a pencil).

G4C02 Which of the following should be installed if a properly operating amateur station is interfering with a nearby telephone?

A. An RFI filter on the transmitter
B. An RFI filter at the affected telephone
C. A high pass filter on the transmitter
D. A high pass filter at the affected telephone

B If you or your neighbor are experiencing telephone interference, the problem can often be cured by inserting an RFI filter directly at the telephone. RFI filters are available at many consumer electronic stores and can be installed by the telephone owner. If the interference persists, have a qualified repair technician or the telephone company check the phone lines and telephone performance, in case there is a problem later.

**Figure G4-5 —
This telephone interference filter has modular connectors to simplify installation right at the telephone.**

G4C03 What sound is heard from a public-address system if there is interference from a nearby single-sideband phone transmitter?

A. A steady hum whenever the transmitter is on the air
B. On-and-off humming or clicking
C. Distorted speech
D. Clearly audible speech

C A public-address system can sometimes rectify (detect) RF signals in much the same way that a radio does. The audio signal is then amplified by the audio device resulting in interference. The amateur's voice will be heard, but it will be highly distorted.

G4C04 **What is the effect on a public-address system if there is interference from nearby CW transmitter?**

A. On-and-off humming or clicking
B. A CW signal at a nearly pure audio frequency
C. A chirpy CW signal
D. Severely distorted audio

A A public-address system can sometimes rectify (detect) RF signals in much the same way that a radio does. The audio signal is then amplified by the audio device resulting in interference. An amateur's CW transmission will be heard as on-and-off humming or clicking.

G4C05 **What might be the problem if you receive an RF burn when touching your equipment while transmitting on a HF band, assuming the equipment is connected to a ground rod?**

A. Flat braid rather than round wire has been used for the ground wire
B. Insulated wire has been used for the ground wire
C. The ground rod is resonant
D. The ground wire is resonant

D One purpose of an amateur station's RF ground wire is to make sure that unwanted signals, such as those picked up from your own transmissions, are directed to ground instead of flowing on or between pieces of equipment. If the ground wire is long enough to be resonant on one or more bands, however, it will not conduct the RF to ground, allowing it to present RF voltages on the chassis of your equipment or microphone, possibly causing an RF burn if it is touched when you are transmitting.

G4C06 **Which of the following is an important reason to have a good station ground?**

A. To reduce the likelihood of RF burns
B. To reduce the likelihood of electrical shock
C. To reduce interference
D. All of these answers are correct

D The purpose of a ground is to conduct any undesired RF signals, electrical noise or even electrical power to ground, and to prevent electrical shock. (See also the discussion for question G4C05.)

G4C07 **What is one good way to avoid stray RF energy in an amateur station?**

A. Keep the station's ground wire as short as possible
B. Install an RF filter in series with the ground wire
C. Use a ground loop for best conductivity
D. Install a few ferrite beads on the ground wire where it connects to your station

A If a ground wire is longer than $\frac{1}{10}$ of a wavelength it can act as an antenna at that frequency or present a high impedance to RF signals. This allows unwanted RF signals to be present in your station. The most effective ground wire will be a short one leading directly from your equipment chassis to a good earth ground.

G4C08 **Which of the following is a reason to place ferrite beads around audio cables to reduce common mode RF interference?**

A. They act as a series inductor
B. They act as a shunt capacitor*
C. They lower the impedance of the cable
D. They increase the admittance of the cable

A Ferrite beads are made of a magnetic material that concentrates magnetic fields around a wire, increasing its natural inductance just as a magnetic core increases the inductance of a coil. This increased inductance presents a reactance to common-mode RF current (current flowing on all conductors in a cable or on the outside of a cable shield), preventing it from flowing on the wire or cable or at least reducing it. This is often sufficient to eliminate RF interference.

G4C09 Which of the following statements about station grounding is true?

A. The chassis of each piece of station equipment should be tied together with high-impedance conductors

B. If the chassis of all station equipment is connected with a good conductor, there is no need to tie them to an earth ground

C. RF hot spots can occur in a station located above the ground floor if the equipment is grounded by a long ground wire

D. A ground loop is an effective way to ground station equipment

C A ground wire that is long enough to act like an antenna or present a high impedance at some frequencies often results in "RF hot spots," a common problem with stations located above the ground floor. Answer choice C is correct. (See also the discussion for question G4C07.)

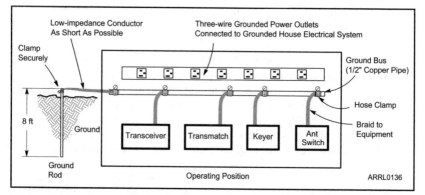

Figure G4-6 — You can make an effective station ground by connecting all equipment to a ground bus. A length of ½ inch copper pipe along the back of your operating desk or table makes a good ground bus. Heavy copper braid, such as the outer braid from RG-8 coaxial cable makes a good, flexible strap to connect each piece of equipment to the ground bus. The whole system then connects to a good earth ground — an 8-foot ground rod located as close to the station as possible is the minimum ground you should use. More than one ground rod may be needed in some locations.

G4C10 Which of the following is covered in the National Electrical Code?

A. Acceptable bandwidth limits

B. Acceptable modulation limits

C. Electrical safety inside the ham shack

D. RF exposure limits of the human body

C The National Electrical Code covers the wiring of electrical devices, including minimum conductor sizes for antennas, grounding conductors and general electrical safety.

G4C11 **Which of the following can cause unintended rectification of RF signal energy and can result in interference to your station as well as nearby radio and TV receivers?**

A. Induced currents in conductors that are in poor electrical contact
B. Induced voltages in conductors that are in good electrical contact
C. Capacitive coupling of the RF signal to ground
D. Excessive standing wave ratio (SWR) of the transmission line system

A Anywhere there are electrical conductors with a poor electrical connection between them, there is the possibility of an RF signal being rectified by this "natural" diode. Weathered joints between sections of TV mast, wire fence and fence stakes, sections of metal rain gutter can all result in a poor electrical connection between those joints. The lengths of metal conductor on either side of the joint can act as antenna elements, picking up RF energy and feeding it to the rectifier. The resulting nonlinear current is rich in harmonic energy, which is then reradiated by the same conductors and picked up by nearby receivers. This type of interference can be particularly difficult to locate and cure.

G4C12 **What is one cause of broadband radio frequency interference at an amateur radio station?**

A. Not using a balun or line isolator to feed balanced antennas
B. Lack of rectification of the transmitter's signal in power conductors
C. Arcing at a poor electrical connection
D. The use of horizontal, rather than vertical antennas

C An arc, such as in motors or at the contacts of electrical equipment, is rich in harmonic energy, even though the primary current may be dc or 60 Hz ac. The resulting RF harmonics can be radiated by the power wiring as broadband noise heard by nearby receivers. Broadband noise can also be caused by intermittent or poor contacts in RF grounds, such as in your own station.

G4C13 How can a ground loop be avoided?

A. Series connect all ground conductors
B. Connect the AC neutral conductor to the ground wire
C. Avoid using lock washers and star washers in making ground connections
D. Connect all ground conductors to a single point

D A ground loop is an undesirable condition in which electrical currents flow to ground through unwanted paths. Avoid ground loops by always providing a single direct path from the equipment chassis to ground. If you connected a second wire to a different ground from another point in the circuit, you could create a condition in which current circulates through the wires and the two ground points. Don't connect the ground wire from one piece of equipment to the next in a series chain, eventually going to the earth ground connection, because this is a good way to create a ground loop. (See Figure G4-6, with the discussion for question G4C09.) The National Electrical Code requires that all earth grounds be connected by conductors. It is a good idea to use star washers or lock washers with any bolts you use to make ground connections, because the teeth on the wires will dig into the conductors and create a good electrical connection. The proper way to create an RF ground for your station is to connect the ground conductors from each piece of equipment to a single point and then connect that point to a good earth ground.

G4D Speech processors; S meters; common connectors

G4D01 What is the reason for using a properly adjusted speech processor with a single-sideband phone transmitter?

A. It reduces average transmitter power requirements
B. It reduces unwanted noise pickup from the microphone
C. It improves voice-frequency fidelity
D. It improves signal intelligibility at the receiver

D A speech processor can improve signal intelligibility by raising average power without increasing peak envelope power (PEP). It does this by bringing up low signal levels while not increasing high signal levels. As a result, the average signal level is higher. A speech processor does not increase the transmitter output PEP.

G4D02 **Which of the following describes how a speech processor affects a transmitted single sideband signal?**

A. It increases the peak power
B. It increases the average power
C. It reduces harmonic distortion
D. It reduces intermodulation distortion

B A speech processor can improve signal intelligibility by raising average power without increasing peak envelope power (PEP). It does this by bringing up low signal levels while not increasing high signal levels. As a result, the average signal level is higher. A speech processor does not increase the output PEP.

Figure G4-7 — A typical SSB voice-modulated signal might have an envelope similar to the oscilloscope display shown at A. The RF amplitude (current or voltage) is on the vertical axis, and the time sweep is on the horizontal axis. After speech processing, the envelope pattern might look like the display at B. The average power of the processed signal has increased, but the PEP has not changed.

G4D03 **Which of the following can be the result of an incorrectly adjusted speech processor?**

A. Distorted speech
B. Splatter
C. Excessive background pickup
D. All of these answers are correct

D Proper adjustment of a speech processor is important to ensure your transmitted signal is not distorted and free of spurious signals. Increasing the amount of processing too far causes your speech to be distorted. Processors that amplify softer speech components more than loud ones will also pick up background noise from fans and other radios and combine them with your desired speech. Another common result of too much processing is overdriving the transmitter output stages, causing interference ("splatter") to signals on nearby frequencies. Read the owner's manual for your radio and learn to operate its speech processor correctly.

G4D04   **What does an S-meter measure?**

A. Conductance
B. Impedance
C. Received signal strength
D. Transmitter power output

C   An S meter measures received signal strength.

G4D05   **How does an S-meter reading of 20 db over S-9 compare to an S-9 signal, assuming a properly calibrated S meter?**

A. It is 10 times weaker
B. It is 20 times weaker
C. It is 20 times stronger
D. It is 100 times stronger

D   A theoretical, ideal S meter operates on a logarithmic scale, indicating one S unit of change for a four-times increase or decrease in power. (This is a 6-dB change in power.) In real life, S meters are only calibrated to this standard in the middle of their range (if at all). Above S9, theoretically corresponding to a 50 μV input signal, S meters are calibrated in dB. In the example of this question, a signal 20 dB stronger than S9 is 100 times stronger than S9.

G4D06   **Where is an S-meter generally found?**

A. In a receiver
B. In a SWR bridge
C. In a transmitter
D. In a conductance bridge

A   An S meter measures received signal strength and so is found in a receiver or the receive circuits of a transceiver.

G4D07   **Which of the following describes a Type-N connector?**

A. A moisture resistant RF connector useful to 10 GHz
B. A small bayonet connector used for data circuits
C. A threaded connector used for hydraulic systems
D. An audio connector used in surround sound installations

A   Type N connectors are connectors for coaxial cable used at HF, VHF, UHF and microwave frequencies to 10 GHz. The Type N connector shell is threaded like a PL-259, but the special design of its body presents the same 50 Ω impedance as coaxial cable so no signals are reflected or lost at the junction of connector and feed line. Type N connectors also have special gaskets built-in so that they are waterproof without additional tape or sleeving.

G4D08 Which of the following connectors would be a good choice for a serial data port?

A. PL-259
B. Type N
C. Type SMA
D. DB-9

D RS-232 serial data interfaces are quite common in amateur equipment. The most common connector used for these interfaces is the D-style DB-9, a 9-pin male or female connector. These connectors are usually found on PC equipment as COM ports.

G4D09 Which of these connector types is commonly used for RF service at frequencies up to 150 MHz?

A. Octal
B. RJ-11
C. UHF
D. DB-25

C The UHF connector family includes the PL-259 cable plug and SO-239 chassis-mounted socket. It is the most popular type of RF connector used on amateur equipment.

Figure G4-8 — This photo shows some common coaxial-cable connectors. At the left, a BNC connector pair. Many handheld radios use BNC connectors. They are popular when a weatherproof connector is needed for RG-58 sized cable. In the center, a pair of N connectors. These are often used for UHF equipment because of their low loss. Type N connectors provide a weatherproof connector for RG-8 sized cables. At the right, a PL-259 coaxial connector and its mating SO-239 chassis connector. Most HF equipment uses these connectors. They are designed for use with RG-8 sized cables, although reducing adapters are available for smaller-diameter cables such as RG-58 and RG-59. Although the PL-259 is sometimes called a "UHF connector," it is seldom used on UHF equipment because it is considered to have too much loss for UHF.

G4D10 Which of these connector types is commonly used for audio signals in amateur radio stations?

A. PL-259
B. BNC
C. RCA Phono
D. Type N

C The RCA phono connector is the most common audio signal connector for consumer electronics and a great deal of amateur equipment. The connector's name derives from its use by the RCA Company for audio connectors and its subsequent popularity for the connection of phonographs to amplifiers and receivers.

G4D11 What is the main reason to use keyed connectors over non-keyed types?

A. Prevention of use by unauthorized persons
B. Reduced chance of damage due to incorrect mating
C. Higher current carrying capacity
D. All of these choices are correct

B A keyed connector has asymmetrical arrangement of contacts or body shapes that allows the connectors to be inserted in only one orientation. This prevents reversed or improper circuit connections that lead to improper operation or damage to the equipment. Do not force keyed connectors together if they are not oriented properly.

G4E HF mobile radio installations; emergency and battery powered operation

G4E01 Which of the following emission types are permissible while operating HF mobile?

A. CW
B. SSB
C. FM
D. All of these choices are correct

D There are no mode limitations on HF mobile operation.

G4E02 What is alternator whine?

A. A DC emission from the alternator
B. A constant pitched tone or buzz in transmitted or received audio that occurs whenever the ignition key is in the on position
C. A tone or buzz in transmitted or received audio that varies with engine speed
D. A mechanical sound from the alternator indicating current overload

C The alternator in a motor vehicle is a dc generator that uses brushes or switches to convert the ac current into dc that can charge the battery and supply the vehicle's electrical systems. The current pulses can be quite large and may cause voltage spikes or surges on the vehicle's power wiring at the frequency of the alternator's rotation. If not filtered out, these will cause an audio whine or tone in received or transmitted audio that follows the alternator's speed. Since the alternator is driven by a belt connected to the engine, the alternator whine will also follow engine speed.

G4E03 **Which of the following power connections would be the best for a 100-watt HF mobile installation?**

A. A direct, fused connection to the battery using heavy gauge wire
B. A direct, fused connection to the alternator or generator using heavy gauge wire
C. A direct, fused connection to the battery using resistor wire
D. A direct, fused connection to the alternator or generator using resistor wire

A   When you are making the power connections for your 100-watt HF radio for mobile operation, you should connect both wires directly to the battery terminals. Remember that both leads should have fuses, placed as close to the battery as possible.

Figure G4-9 — This drawing shows a typical mobile-transceiver-installation wiring diagram.

G4E04   **Why is it best NOT to draw the DC power for a 100-watt HF transceiver from an automobile's cigarette lighter socket?**

A. The socket is not wired with an RF-shielded power cable
B. The socket's wiring may be inadequate for the current being drawn by the transceiver
C. The DC polarity of the socket is reversed from the polarity of modern HF transceivers
D. The power from the socket is never adequately filtered for HF transceiver operation

B   The cigarette lighter wiring is adequate for your low-power hand-held radio but probably is not adequate for a full-power HF rig drawing 20 amps when transmitting. When you are making the power connections for your 100-watt HF radio for mobile operation, you should connect both wires directly to the battery terminals. Remember that both leads should have fuses, placed as close to the battery as possible.

G4E05 **Which of the following most limits the effectiveness of an HF mobile transceiver operating in the 75 meter band?**

A. "Picket Fencing" signal variation
B. The wire gauge of the DC power line to the transceiver
C. The HF mobile antenna system
D. FCC rules limiting mobile output power on the 75 meter band

C   HF mobile antenna systems are the most limiting factor for effective operation of your station. Placing even an 8-foot vertical antenna on top of a small car makes a dangerously tall system. If you have a taller vehicle, this kind of antenna is almost out of the question. Some type of inductive loading to shorten the length is then required. For operation on the 75-meter band this compromise results in a relatively inefficient antenna system.

G4E06 **Which of the following is true of an emergency generator installation?**

A. The generator should be located in a well ventilated area
B. The generator should be insulated from ground
C. Fuel should be stored near the generator for rapid refueling in case of an emergency
D. All of these choices are correct

A   Carbon monoxide and other exhaust fumes can accumulate in your garage, basement or other confined living area, so ventilation is very important. Be sure not to place generators near air intakes or vents, as well.

G4E07 **When might a lead-acid storage battery give off explosive hydrogen gas?**

A. When stored for long periods of time
B. When being discharged
C. When being charged
D. When not placed on a level surface

C   You need to keep your lead-acid battery charged at all times for use in an emergency. A by-product of charging your battery is the release of hydrogen gas that can explode if ignited by a spark. A well-ventilated area is essential.

G4E08 What is the name of the process by which sunlight is changed directly into electricity?

A. Photovoltaic conversion
B. Photon emission
C. Photosynthesis
D. Photon decomposition

A   Natural sources of energy are becoming more economical and more practical as a way to power your station. Photovoltaic conversion by solar cells and panels converts sunlight into dc electricity.

G4E09 What is the approximate open-circuit voltage from a modern, well illuminated photovoltaic cell?

A. 0.02 VDC
B. 0.5 VDC
C. 0.2 VDC
D. 1.38 VDC

B   Each photovoltaic cell produces about 0.5 volt in full sunlight if there is no load connected to the cell. The size or surface area of the cell determines the maximum current that the cell can supply.

G4E10 Which of these materials is used as the active element of a solar cell?

A. Doped Silicon
B. Nickel Hydride
C. Doped Platinum
D. Aluminum nitride

A   A solar cell is actually nothing more than a diode with a PN junction. The P- and N-type material are created by adding impurities (doping) to silicon, just as for semiconductor components. However, the cell has a large surface area so that photons of sunlight can penetrate the cell and cause current to flow across the junction.

G4E11 **Which of the following is a disadvantage to using wind power as the primary source of power for an emergency station?**

A. The conversion efficiency from mechanical energy to electrical energy is less than 2 percent
B. The voltage and current ratings of such systems are not compatible with amateur equipment
C. A large energy storage system is needed to supply power when the wind is not blowing
D. All of these choices are correct

C Wind-powered systems, while complex in design and construction, provide free energy after the initial cost. Just like solar-powered systems, wind systems need to have a storage battery to supply electricity when the wind is not blowing.

G4E12 **Which of the following is a primary reason for not placing a gasoline-fueled generator inside an occupied area?**

A. Danger of carbon monoxide poisoning
B. Danger of engine over torque
C. Lack of oxygen for adequate combustion
D. Lack of nitrogen for adequate combustion

A Carbon monoxide and other exhaust fumes can accumulate in your garage, basement or other confined living area, so ventilation is very important. Be sure not to place generators near air intakes or vents, as well.

G4E13   Why would it be unwise to power your station by back feeding the output of a gasoline generator into your house wiring by connecting the generator through an AC wall outlet?

A. It might present a hazard for electric company workers
B. It is prone to RF interference
C. It may disconnect your RF ground
D. None of the above; this is an excellent expedient

A   It is common to use a generator to provide power for other household uses when the commercial ac power goes off for some reason. The proper way to make use of generator power for household use is to have a qualified electrician install a transfer switch in the electrical power feed to the house. The transfer switch ensures that your home's circuits are connected to the power line or the generator but never both at the same time.

As a quick way to power the house, some people have made a power cord that will plug the generator output into an ac wall outlet in the house, thus feeding power from the generator throughout the house. This practice, called "back feeding," is dangerous for several reasons. First, it is very dangerous for the power company workers, who may suddenly find that a "dead" line has power applied! Small portable generators do not generally produce enough current to operate appliances, lights and other household loads. Trying to power your house with such a generator can lead to an overloaded generator, and damaged equipment. In addition, if the commercial ac power is restored to your house while your generator is connected, it may damage or destroy the generator.

Electrical Principles

Your General class exam (Element 3) will consist of 35 questions taken from the General class question pool as prepared by the Volunteer Examiner Coordinators' Question Pool Committee. A certain number of questions are taken from each of the 10 subelements. There will be 3 questions from the subelement shown in this chapter. These questions are divided into 3 groups, labeled G5A through G5C.

G5A Resistance; reactance; inductance; capacitance; impedance; impedance matching

G5A01 What is impedance?
A. The electric charge stored by a capacitor
B. The inverse of resistance
C. The opposition to the flow of current in an AC circuit
D. The force of repulsion between two similar electric fields

C Impedance is the opposition to the flow of current in an alternating current (ac) circuit. Capacitive reactance, inductive reactance and resistance are all types of impedance.

G5A02 What is reactance?
A. Opposition to the flow of direct current caused by resistance
B. Opposition to the flow of alternating current caused by capacitance or inductance
C. A property of ideal resistors in AC circuits
D. A large spark produced at switch contacts when an inductor is deenergized

B The opposition to the flow of ac current caused by inductors and capacitors in an alternating current (ac) circuit is referred to as reactance. Reactance is one component of impedance, along with resistance.

G5A03 Which of the following causes opposition to the flow of
alternating current in an inductor?

A. Conductance
B. Reluctance
C. Admittance
D. Reactance

D The opposition to the flow of current in an alternating current (ac) circuit
caused by an inductor is referred to as inductive reactance, or simply reactance.
Reactance is one component of impedance, along with resistance.

G5A04 Which of the following causes opposition to the flow of
alternating current in a capacitor?

A. Conductance
B. Reluctance
C. Reactance
D. Admittance

C The opposition to the flow of current in an alternating current (ac) circuit
caused by a capacitor is referred to as capacitive reactance, or simply reactance.
Reactance is one component of impedance, along with resistance.

G5A05 How does a coil react to AC?

A. As the frequency of the applied AC increases, the reactance
   decreases
B. As the amplitude of the applied AC increases, the reactance increases
C. As the amplitude of the applied AC increases, the reactance
   decreases
D. As the frequency of the applied AC increases, the reactance increases

D A coil is also known as an inductor. The opposition to the flow of current
caused by the coil in an alternating current (ac) circuit is referred to as inductive
reactance. Inductive reactance increases as the ac frequency increases.

G5A06 How does a capacitor react to AC?

A. As the frequency of the applied AC increases, the reactance
   decreases
B. As the frequency of the applied AC increases, the reactance increases
C. As the amplitude of the applied AC increases, the reactance increases
D. As the amplitude of the applied AC increases, the reactance
   decreases

A The opposition to the flow of current caused by a capacitor in an alternating
current (ac) circuit is referred to as capacitive reactance. This reactance decreases
as the ac frequency increases.

G5A07 **What happens when the impedance of an electrical load is equal to the internal impedance of the power source?**

    A. The source delivers minimum power to the load

    B. The electrical load is shorted

    C. No current can flow through the circuit

    D. The source can deliver maximum power to the load

D   A power source delivers maximum power to a load when the impedance of the load is equal to (matched to) the impedance of the source. When the impedances are not matched, the power source cannot transfer as much power to the load. This is true for both dc power sources (such as batteries or power supplies) and ac power sources (such as transmitters).

G5A08 **Why is impedance matching important?**

    A. So the source can deliver maximum power to the load

    B. So the load will draw minimum power from the source

    C. To ensure that there is less resistance than reactance in the circuit

    D. To ensure that the resistance and reactance in the circuit are equal

A   See the discussion for question G5A07.

G5A09 **What unit is used to measure reactance?**

    A. Farad

    B. Ohm

    C. Ampere

    D. Siemens

B   The ohm is the unit used to measure any opposition to the flow of current. In an ac circuit, this opposition is referred to as impedance, and includes both reactance and resistance.

G5A10 **What unit is used to measure impedance?**

    A. Volt

    B. Ohm

    C. Ampere

    D. Watt

B   The ohm is the unit used to measure any opposition to the flow of current. In an ac circuit, this opposition is referred to as impedance, and includes both reactance and resistance.

G5A11 **Why should core saturation of a conventional impedance matching transformer be avoided?**

A. Harmonics and distortion could result
B. Magnetic flux would increase with frequency
C. RF susceptance would increase
D. Temporary changes of the core permeability could result

A By using a magnetic core in a transformer, the ability of the windings to transfer magnetic energy is increased because the core focuses the magnetic field or flux inside. Saturation occurs when the current in the windings creates more magnetic flux than the core can store. Beyond that level of current, the waveform of the energy being transferred through the transformer is distorted, creating harmonics and other spurious signals. The core can overheat and be damaged, as well. To prevent saturation, use a sufficiently large core to handle all of the expected magnetic flux.

G5A12 **What is one reason to use an impedance matching transformer?**

A. To reduce power dissipation in the transmitter
B. To maximize the transfer of power
C. To minimize SWR at the antenna
D. To minimize SWR in the transmission line

B An impedance matching transformer changes the ratio of voltage and current between the load and source. Since impedance is the ratio of voltage and current, the transformer can also match different impedances. Matching impedances also maximizes power transfer between the source and load. (See also the discussion for question G5A07.)

G5A13 **Which of the following devices can be used for impedance matching at radio frequencies?**

A. A transformer
B. A Pi-network
C. A length of transmission line
D. All of these choices are correct

D All of these can alter the ratio of voltage and current in a circuit, effectively changing the impedance as well. (See the discussion for question G5A12.) A Pi-network is an LC-circuit that uses the exchange of stored energy between the inductors and capacitors to transform the ratio of voltage and current (impedance) between the input and output. Special lengths of transmission lines (called "stubs") set up patterns of reflections in the feed line that cancel the reflections from a mismatched load, making the load impedance appear as if it was the same as that of the feed line.

G5A14 Which of the following describes one method of impedance matching between two AC circuits?

    A. Insert an LC network between the two circuits
    B. Reduce the power output of the first circuit
    C. Increase the power output of the first circuit
    D. Insert a circulator between the two circuits

A An LC network, such as the Pi-network of question G5A13, uses the exchange of stored energy between the inductors and capacitors to transform the ratio of voltage and current (impedance) between the input and output. Common examples of impedance matching LC networks are the L-, T-, and Pi-network, named for the arrangement of the components on a schematic.

G5B The Decibel; current and voltage dividers; electrical power calculations; sine wave root-mean-square (RMS) values; PEP calculations

G5B01 A two-times increase or decrease in power results in a change of how many dB?

    A. 2 dB
    B. 3 dB
    C. 6 dB
    D. 12 dB

B The decibel scale is a logarithmic scale in which a two-times increase (or decrease) in power is represented by 3 dB. The mathematical formula for the decibel scale for power is:

$$dB = 10 \times \log_{10} \left(\frac{P_2}{P_1} \right)$$

where:

P_1 = reference power and P_2 = power being compared to the reference value.

$$dB = 10 \times \log_{10} \left(\frac{2}{1} \right) = 10 \times \log_{10} (2) = 10 \times 0.3 = 3 \, dB$$

Table G5B01

Some Common Decibel Values and Power Ratio Equivalents

dB	P2 / P1	dB	P2 / P1
20	100 (10^2)	−3	0.5
10	10 (10^1)	−6	0.25
6	4	−10	0.1 (10^{-1})
3	2	−20	0.01 (10^{-2})
0	1		

G5B02 **How does the total current relate to the individual currents in each branch of a parallel circuit?**

A. It equals the average of each branch current
B. It decreases as more parallel resistors are added to the circuit
C. It equals the sum of the currents through each branch
D. It is the sum of the reciprocal of each individual voltage drop

C In a circuit with several parallel branches, the total current flowing into the junction of the branches is equal to the sum of the current through each branch.

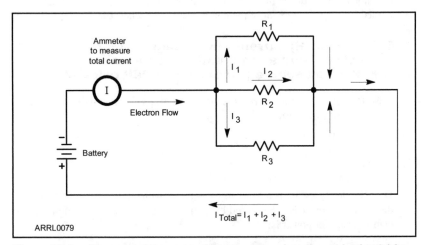

Figure G5-1 — The sum of the current flowing into a junction point (node) in a circuit must be equal to the current flowing out of the junction point (node). This principle is called Kirchhoff's Current Law, named for Gustav Kirchhoff, the German scientist who discovered it. (This figure shows actual electron flow, the opposite of conventional current.)

G5B03 How many watts of electrical power are used if 400 VDC is supplied to an 800-ohm load?

    A. 0.5 watts

    B. 200 watts

    C. 400 watts

    D. 3200 watts

B Since $P = I \times E$ and $I = E/R$, the power in a circuit also can be expressed as

$$P = \frac{E \times E}{R}$$

In this case:

$$P = \frac{E \times E}{R} = \frac{400 \times 400}{800} = \frac{160,000}{800} = 200 \text{ W}$$

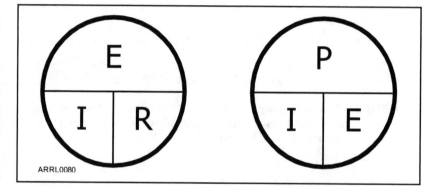

ARRL0080

Figure G5-2 — The "Ohm's Law Circle" and the "Power Circle" will help you remember the equations that include voltage, current, resistance and power. Cover the letter representing the unknown quantity to find an equation to calculate that quantity. If you cover the I in the Ohm's Law Circle, you are left with E/R. If you cover the P in the Power Circle, you are left with I × E. Combining these terms, you can write the equation to calculate power when you know the voltage and the resistance.

G5B04 **How many watts of electrical power are used by a 12-VDC light bulb that draws 0.2 amperes?**

A. 2.4 watts
B. 24 watts
C. 6 watts
D. 60 watts

A Use the Power Circle drawing to find the equation to calculate power. The power in a circuit is equal to the voltage times the current:

$P = I \times E = 0.2 \times 12 = 2.4$ W

G5B05 **How many watts are being dissipated when a current of 7.0 milliamperes flows through 1.25 kilohms?**

A. Approximately 61 milliwatts
B. Approximately 39 milliwatts
C. Approximately 11 milliwatts
D. Approximately 9 milliwatts

A Use the Ohm's Law Circle and Power Circle drawings to find the equations to calculate power. Since $P = I \times E$ and $E = R \times I$, the power in a circuit can also be expressed as $P = I \times I \times R$.

$P = I \times I \times R = 0.007 \times 0.007 \times 1250 = 0.06125$ W $= 61.25$ mW

Note: Remember that 7 milliamperes is equal to 0.007 ampere, 1.25 kilohms is equal to 1250 ohms and 0.06125 watt is equal to approximately 61 milliwatts.

G5B06 **What is the output PEP from a transmitter if an oscilloscope measures 200 volts peak-to-peak across a 50-ohm dummy load connected to the transmitter output?**

A. 1.4 watts
B. 100 watts
C. 353.5 watts
D. 400 watts

B PEP is the output power measured at the peak of the RF cycle at the peak of the signal's envelope and is equal to:

$$PEP = \frac{(\text{Peak envelope voltage} \times 0.707)^2}{R}$$

$$\text{Peak envelope voltage} = \frac{\text{Peak} - \text{to} - \text{peak envelope voltage}}{2} \text{ , so}$$

$$PEP = \frac{(100 \times 0.707)^2}{50} = 100 \text{ W}$$

G5B07   Which measurement of an AC signal is equivalent to a DC voltage of the same value?

A. The peak-to-peak value
B. The peak value
C. The RMS value
D. The reciprocal of the RMS value

C   RMS, or root mean square, voltage values convert a constantly-varying ac voltage to the equivalent of a constant dc voltage. The RMS value of an ac voltage is the value that would deliver the same amount of power to a load as a dc voltage of the same value.

G5B08   What is the peak-to-peak voltage of a sine wave that has an RMS voltage of 120 volts?

A. 84.8 volts
B. 169.7 volts
C. 240.0 volts
D. 339.4 volts

D   If you know the RMS voltage and want to know the peak value, multiply the RMS by the square root of 2 (which is 1.414). If you want to know peak-to-peak, double the result. In this case:

$120 \times 1.414 \times 2 = 339.4$ V

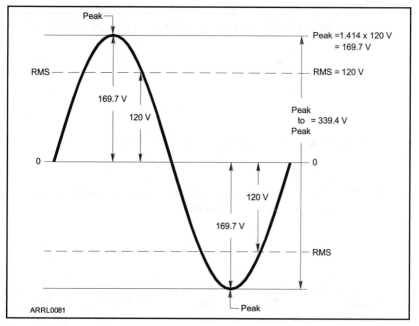

Figure G5-3 — An illustration of the relationship between ac measurements for sine wave waveforms. RMS value conversions assume that the waveform is a sine wave. Different conversion values are required for other waveform shapes, such as square or triangle waves.

G5B09 **What is the RMS voltage of sine wave with a value of 17 volts peak?**

    A. 8.5 volts
    B. 12 volts
    C. 24 volts
    D. 34 volts

B   If you know the peak voltage, you can find the RMS value by multiplying the peak voltage by 0.707 (which is the same as dividing by the square root of 2). In this case:

$17 \times 0.707 = 12$ V

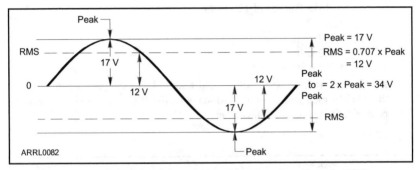

Figure G5-4 — An example of the relationship of peak voltage to RMS.

G5B10   This question has been withdrawn.

G5B11   **What is the ratio of peak envelope power to average power for an unmodulated carrier?**

    A. .707
    B. 1.00
    C. 1.414
    D. 2.00

B   It's 1.0 because for an unmodulated carrier all RF cycles have the same voltage, meaning that the envelope's average and peak values are the same.

G5B12 **What would be the voltage across a 50-ohm dummy load dissipating 1200 watts?**

    A. 173 volts
    B. 245 volts
    C. 346 volts
    D. 692 volts

B   It's 245 V because

$$P = \frac{E^2}{R}, \text{ so } 1200 = \frac{E^2}{50} \text{ and}$$

$$E = \sqrt{1200 \times 50} = \sqrt{60,000} = 245 \text{ V}$$

This is the RMS voltage across the 50 Ω load.

G5B13 What percentage of power loss would result from a transmission line loss of 1 dB?

    A. 10.9 %
    B. 12.2 %
    C. 20.5 %
    D. 25.9 %

C The decibel scale is a logarithmic scale in which a two-times increase (or decrease) in power is represented by 3 dB. The mathematical formula for the decibel scale for power is:

$$dB = 10 \times \log_{10}\left(\frac{P_2}{P_1}\right)$$

where:

P_1 = reference power and P_2 = power being compared to the reference value.

In this question we are told that the transmission line to an antenna results in a signal loss of 1 dB. We can use the decibel equation to calculate the power that reaches the antenna through this feed line, and from that we can calculate the power lost in the feed line. If we assume a transmitter power of 100 W, then the resulting answer will be the percentage of the original power that is lost in the feed line. First we will solve the decibel equation for P2, the power that reaches the antenna.

$$dB = 10 \times \log_{10}\left(\frac{P_2}{P_1}\right)$$

$$\frac{dB}{10} = \log_{10}\left(\frac{P_2}{P_1}\right)$$

$$\log_{10}{}^{-1}\left(\frac{dB}{10}\right) = \left(\frac{P_2}{P_1}\right)$$

Note: The notation that shows the logarithm raised to the negative 1 power means the antilog, or inverse logarithm. On some scientific calculators this button is also labeled 10x, which means "raise 10 to the power of this value." The decibel value is given as a loss of 1 dB, so we will write that as –1 dB.

$$P_1 \log_{10}{}^{-1}\left(\frac{dB}{10}\right) = P_2 = 100 \text{ W} \times \log_{10}{}^{-1}\left(\frac{-1 \text{ dB}}{10}\right)$$

$$= 100 \text{ W} \times 0.794 = 79.4 \text{ W}$$

If 79.4 W is the power actually reaching the antenna, then we can calculate the lost power by subtracting this value from the original power: 100 W – 79.4 W = 20.6 W. Because we used 100 W as the reference power, this value is the percentage of the original power that is lost in our feed line, when it has a loss of 1 dB. The percentage of the power lost in this feed line is 20.6%.

G5B14   What is the output PEP from a transmitter if an oscilloscope measures 500 volts peak-to-peak across a 50-ohm resistor connected to the transmitter output?

A. 8.75 watts
B. 625 watts
C. 2500 watts
D. 5000 watts

B   To figure this out, use the formula

$$PEP = \frac{E_{RMS}^2}{R}$$

The question gives peak-to-peak voltage, which must be converted to RMS by

$$E_{RMS} = 0.707 \times E_{PEAK} = 0.707 \times \frac{E_{PK-PK}}{2} \quad , so$$

$$PEP = \frac{E_{RMS}^2}{R} = \frac{\left(\dfrac{500}{2} \times 0.707\right)^2}{50} = 625 \text{ W}$$

G5B15   What is the output PEP of an unmodulated carrier if an average reading wattmeter connected to the transmitter output indicates 1060 watts?

A. 530 watts
B. 1060 watts
C. 1500 watts
D. 2120 watts

B   The PEP and average power of an unmodulated carrier are the same. For an unmodulated carrier all RF cycles have the same voltage, meaning that the envelope's average and peak values are the same.

G5C Resistors, capacitors, and inductors in series and parallel; transformers

G5C01 What causes a voltage to appear across the secondary winding of a transformer when an AC voltage source is connected across its primary winding?

A. Capacitive coupling
B. Displacement current coupling
C. Mutual inductance
D. Mutual capacitance

C A transformer consists of two coils (windings) sharing a common core so that the flux from one winding is shared by both windings. An ac signal in the input coil, called the primary winding produces an ac signal in the output coil, called the secondary winding. The core material might be layers of steel, a powdered iron mixture, some other magnetic material, or even air. The coupling between the primary and secondary windings is called mutual inductance.

When a current flows through the primary winding it creates a magnetic field in the core. That magnetic field changes polarity and strength as the primary ac voltage changes. The changing magnetic field in the common core is shared by the secondary winding, inducing a voltage across the turns of the secondary winding and creating a current in the secondary circuit.

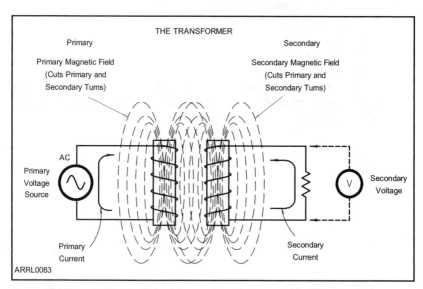

Figure G5-5 — An illustration of how a transformer works. The input of a transformer is called the primary winding, and the output is called the secondary winding. In this drawing separate primary and secondary cores are shown to illustrate how the windings share magnetic flux. In most transformers, both windings are wound on a common core for more complete sharing of flux.

G5C02 **Where is the source of energy normally connected in a transformer?**

A. To the secondary winding
B. To the primary winding
C. To the core
D. To the plates

B   The primary winding is generally considered to be the input. However energy can flow in either direction, primary-to-secondary or secondary-to-primary.

G5C03 **What is current in the primary winding of a transformer called if no load is attached to the secondary?**

A. Magnetizing current
B. Direct current
C. Excitation current
D. Stabilizing current

A   Magnetizing current is the current that creates the magnetic field shared by both windings.

G5C04 **What is the total resistance of three 100-ohm resistors in parallel?**

A. .30 ohms
B. .33 ohms
C. 33.3 ohms
D. 300 ohms

C   To calculate the total resistance of resistors in parallel take the reciprocal of the sum of the resistor's reciprocal values as follows:

$$R = \frac{1}{\frac{1}{100} + \frac{1}{100} + \frac{1}{100}} = \frac{100}{3} = 33.3 \ \Omega$$

G5C05 What is the value of each resistor if three equal value resistors in parallel produce 50 ohms of resistance, and the same three resistors in series produce 450 ohms?

A. 1500 ohms
B. 90 ohms
C. 150 ohms
D. 175 ohms

C For resistors of equal value in parallel, the resulting resistance equals the common resistor value divided by the number of resistors, n:

$$R = \frac{\text{Common Value}}{n}$$

For resistors in series, the resulting resistance equals the sum of the resistor values:

$$R = R1 + R2 + R3 + \ldots = \text{Common Value} \times n$$

In this case, in parallel the total resistance of

$$50 \, \Omega = \frac{\text{Common Value}}{3} \text{, and so Common Value} = 50 \times 3 = 150 \, \Omega$$

In series, the total resistance of

$$450 \, \Omega = \text{Common Value} \times 3 \text{, and so Common Value} = \frac{450}{3} = 150 \, \Omega$$

The common value can be calculated from either equation.

G5C06 **What is the voltage across a 500-turn secondary winding in a transformer if the 2250-turn primary is connected to 120 VAC?**

A. 2370 volts
B. 540 volts
C. 26.7 volts
D. 5.9 volts

C The voltage in the secondary winding of a transformer is equal to the voltage in the primary winding times the ratio of turns in the secondary to the primary.

$$E_S = E_P \times \frac{N_S}{N_P}$$

If the 2250-turn primary is connected to 120 volts ac, the voltage across a 500-turn secondary winding in the transformer is 26.7 volts:

$$E_S = E_P \times \frac{N_S}{N_P} = 120 \text{ V} \times \frac{500}{2250} = 26.7 \text{ V}$$

G5C07 **What is the turns ratio of a transformer used to match an audio amplifier having a 600-ohm output impedance to a speaker having a 4-ohm impedance?**

A. 12.2 to 1
B. 24.4 to 1
C. 150 to 1
D. 300 to 1

A To calculate the turns ratio, take the square root of the impedance ratio:

$$\text{Turns ratio} = \sqrt{\frac{Z_P}{Z_S}} = \sqrt{\frac{600}{4}} = \sqrt{150} = 12.2$$

Z_P is the impedance of the load connected to the primary and Z_S is the load connected to secondary.

G5C08 **What is the equivalent capacitance of two 5000 picofarad capacitors and one 750 picofarad capacitor connected in parallel?**

A. 576.9 picofarads
B. 1733 picofarads
C. 3583 picofarads
D. 10750 picofarads

D To calculate the total capacitance of capacitors in parallel, add the values of the capacitors together:

$$C = C1 + C2 + C3 + \ldots + C_N$$

$$C = 5000 \text{ pF} + 5000 \text{ pF} + 750 \text{ pF} = 10750 \text{ pF}$$

G5C09   What is the capacitance of three 100 microfarad capacitors connected in series?

    A.   .30 microfarads
    B.   .33 microfarads
    C.   33.3 microfarads
    D.   300 microfarads

C   For capacitors of equal value in series, the resulting capacitance equals the common capacitor value divided by the number of capacitors, n:

$$C = \frac{Common\ Value}{n}$$

$$C = \frac{100\ \mu F}{3} = 33.3\ \mu F$$

G5C10   What is the inductance of three 10 millihenry inductors connected in parallel?

    A.   .30 Henrys
    B.   3.3 Henrys
    C.   3.3 millihenrys
    D.   30 millihenrys

C   For inductors of equal value in parallel, the resulting inductance equals the common inductor value divided by the number of inductors, n:

$$L = \frac{Common\ Value}{n}$$

$$L = \frac{10\ mH}{3} = 3.3\ mH$$

G5C11   What is the inductance of a 20 millihenry inductor in series with a 50 millihenry inductor?

    A.   .07 millihenrys
    B.   14.3 millihenrys
    C.   70 millihenrys
    D.   1000 millihenrys

C   For inductors in series, the resulting inductance equals the sum of the inductor values:

$$L = L1 + L2 + L3 + \ldots + L_N$$

$$L = 20\ mH + 50\ mH = 70\ mH$$

G5C12 What is the capacitance of a 20 microfarad capacitor in series with a 50 microfarad capacitor?

- A. .07 microfarads
- B. 14.3 microfarads
- C. 70 microfarads
- D. 1000 microfarads

B To calculate the total capacitance of capacitors in series take the reciprocal of the sum of the capacitor's reciprocal values as follows:

$$C = \frac{1}{\dfrac{1}{C1} + \dfrac{1}{C2} + \dfrac{1}{C3} + \dots + \dfrac{1}{C_N}}$$

In the case of two capacitors in series, the equation simplifies to:

$$C_{total} = \frac{C1 \times C2}{C1 + C2} = \frac{20 \times 50}{20 + 50} = \frac{1000}{70} = 14.3 \, \mu F$$

G5C13 What component should be added to a capacitor in a circuit to increase the circuit capacitance?

- A. An inductor in series
- B. A resistor in series
- C. A capacitor in parallel
- D. A capacitor in series

C Add additional capacitors in parallel to increase the total capacitance.

G5C14 What component should be added to an inductor in a circuit to increase the circuit inductance?

- A. A capacitor in series
- B. A resistor in parallel
- C. An inductor in parallel
- D. An inductor in series

D Add additional inductors in series to increase the total inductance.

G5C15 What is the total resistance of a 10 ohm, a 20 ohm, and a
50 ohm resistor in parallel?

A. 5.9 ohms
B. 0.17 ohms
C. 10000 ohms
D. 80 ohms

A   See the discussion for question G5C04.

$$R = \cfrac{1}{\cfrac{1}{10} + \cfrac{1}{20} + \cfrac{1}{50}} = 5.9 \, \Omega$$

G5C16 What component should be added to an existing resistor in a
circuit to increase circuit resistance?

A. A resistor in parallel
B. A resistor in series
C. A capacitor in series
D. A capacitor in parallel

B   Add additional resistors in series to increase the total resistance.

Circuit Components

Your General class exam (Element 3) will consist of 35 questions taken from the General class question pool as prepared by the Volunteer Examiner Coordinators' Question Pool Committee. A certain number of questions are taken from each of the 10 subelements. There will be 3 questions from the subelement shown in this chapter. These questions are divided into 3 groups, labeled G6A through G6C.

G6A   Resistors; capacitors; inductors

G6A01   What will happen to the resistance if the temperature of a carbon resistor is increased?
A. It will increase by 20% for every 10 degrees centigrade
B. It will stay the same
C. It will change depending on the resistor's temperature coefficient rating
D. It will become time dependent

C   The resistance value of almost any substance changes when heated. The amount of change depends on the resistor's temperature coefficient. Carbon composition resistors usually have a positive temperature coefficient, meaning that as the temperature increases, the resistance value increases.

G6A02 What type of capacitor is often used in power-supply circuits to filter the rectified AC?

    A. Disc ceramic
    B. Vacuum variable
    C. Mica
    D. Electrolytic

D Because electrolytic capacitors can be made with the required high capacitance value in a small package, they are often used in power supply circuits to filter the rectified ac voltage.

Figure G6-1 — Part A shows the construction of an aluminum electrolytic capacitor. Part B shows the construction of a tantalum electrolytic capacitor.

G6A03 Which of the following is the primary advantage of ceramic capacitors?

A. Tight tolerance
B. High stability
C. High capacitance for given volume
D. Comparatively low cost

D All of these choices could be correct, but the primary advantage of ceramic capacitors is that they offer good performance at low cost. Ceramic capacitors are usually used as bypass capacitors that filter out high-frequency ac voltages from dc and low-frequency signal connections.

G6A04 Which of the following is an advantage of an electrolytic capacitor?

A. Tight tolerance
B. Non-polarized
C. High capacitance for given volume
D. Inexpensive RF capacitor

C Electrolytic capacitors are designed to provide large values of capacitance for energy storage and ac voltage filtering. Their construction, shown in Figure G6-1, provides relatively high capacitance in a small volume. The tradeoff is that dc voltage applied to them must always be of the same polarity and the manufacturing technique leads to rather wide variations in capacitance.

G6A05 Which of the following is one effect of lead inductance in a capacitor used at VHF and above?

A. Effective capacitance may be reduced
B. Voltage rating may be reduced
C. ESR may be reduced
D. The polarity of the capacitor might become reversed

A Lead inductance creates a small inductance in series with the capacitor. At low frequencies, lead inductance can be ignored, but at VHF and higher frequencies, the inductive reactance begins to cancel the capacitor's own reactance, reducing the effective capacitance dramatically! Capacitors to be used at these high frequencies must have very short leads.

G6A06 What is the main disadvantage of using a conventional wire-wound resistor in a resonant circuit?

A. The resistor's tolerance value would not be adequate for such a circuit
B. The resistor's inductance could detune the circuit
C. The resistor could overheat
D. The resistor's internal capacitance would detune the circuit

B Wire-wound resistors are made exactly as their name implies. A length of "resistance wire" — usually a nickel chromium, or nichrome alloy — is wound around a ceramic form. The wire has some specific resistance per length of wire, so the length of wire is chosen to give the desired resistance. Because a long length of wire is difficult to accommodate in an electronics circuit, the wire is wound on the form to reduce the overall length of the resistor. The resistor is then coated with a ceramic or other insulating material to protect the wire. If this construction method sounds like an inductor to you, you are absolutely correct! It is not a good idea to use wire-wound resistors in any RF circuits or anywhere that you don't want some extra amount of inductance to be included in the circuit. The extra inductance will detune any resonant circuit of which it is part or add unwanted inductive reactance to signal paths.

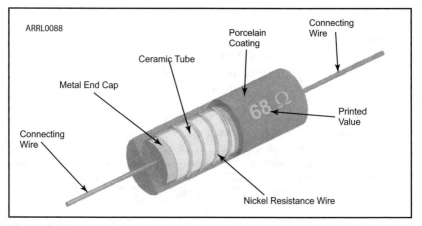

Figure G6-2 — This drawing shows the construction of a simple wire-wound resistor.

G6A07 **What is an advantage of using a ferrite core with a toroidal inductor?**

A. Large values of inductance may be obtained
B. The magnetic properties of the core may be optimized for a specific range of frequencies
C. Most of the magnetic field is contained in the core
D. All of these choices are correct

D   Because a toroid core offers a continuous, circular path for magnetic flux, nearly all of a toroidal inductor's magnetic field is contained inside the core. This gives toroidal inductors a self-shielding property that makes them ideal for use in RF circuits, where you do not want interaction between nearby inductors. Ferrite is a ceramic containing iron compounds. Ferrite and powdered-iron toroid cores both have high permeabilities (the ability to store magnetic energy). That makes it possible to obtain large values of inductance in a relatively small package, as compared to the number of turns that would be required with an air-core inductor. The material used to make the core can be optimized to work best on a specific range of frequencies. All of the answer choices are true statements, so answer D is correct.

G6A08 How should two solenoid inductors be placed so as to minimize their mutual inductance?

A. In line with their winding axis
B. With their winding axes parallel to each other
C. With their winding axes at right angles to each other
D. Within the same shielded enclosure

C An inductor that is formed by winding a coil of wire on a straight coil form of either air or a magnetic material is called a solenoid inductor. The magnetic field associated with a solenoid core extends through the center of the core and then around the outside of the coil. To minimize any interaction between the magnetic fields around solenoid inductors in a circuit, the coils should be placed so that the axes along which the wire is wound are at right angles to each other. (To ensure minimum interaction between solenoid coils you might also have to place each inductor inside its own shielded enclosure.)

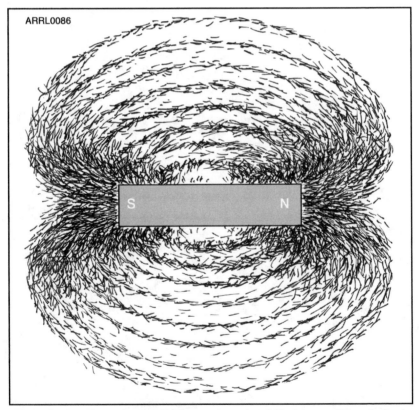

Figure G6-3 — The magnetic field around a solenoid inductor will be similar to the magnetic field around a bar magnet.

G6A09 **Why might it be important to minimize the mutual inductance between two inductors?**

A. To increase the energy transfer between both circuits
B. To reduce or eliminate unwanted coupling
C. To reduce conducted emissions
D. To increase the self-resonant frequency of both inductors

B It is important to minimize any mutual inductance between two inductors because when the magnetic field of one inductor affects the field of another inductor there may be some stray RF coupling between different circuit stages.

G6A10 **What is an effect of inter-turn capacitance in an inductor?**

A. The magnetic field may become inverted
B. The inductor may become self resonant at some frequencies
C. The permeability will increase
D. The voltage rating may be exceeded

B Inter-turn capacitance is created by adjacent turns of wire separated by air or their insulation. Even though the turns of wire are connected, the small separation between the wire surfaces creates a small capacitance. In a coil of many turns, the inter-turn capacitance can become significant. At high frequencies, the combination of the coil's inductance and the inter-turn capacitance can become a series- or parallel-resonant circuit!

G6A11 **What is the common name for a capacitor connected across a transformer secondary that is used to absorb transient voltage spikes?**

A. Clipper capacitor
B. Trimmer capacitor
C. Feedback capacitor
D. Suppressor capacitor

D A suppressor capacitor takes its name from the fact that it suppresses otherwise damaging spikes and surges in a power-supply circuit. The name suppressor capacitor indicates the circuit function that the capacitor serves. It does not identify a particular type of capacitor construction.

Figure G6-4 — This circuit shows the 120-V ac input and transformer for a power supply. The MOV on the transformer primary suppresses transient spikes on the ac line voltage. The suppressor capacitor on the transformer secondary filters any transient voltage that comes through the transformer.

G6A12 **What is the common name for an inductor used to help smooth the DC output from the rectifier in a conventional power supply?**

A. Back EMF choke
B. Repulsion coil
C. Charging inductor
D. Filter choke

D A filter choke is an inductor that is connected in series with the output of a power supply rectifier. It works with the filter capacitor to smooth the pulses of rectifier output into dc. The inductor is called a choke because it "chokes off" the variations in voltage at its input. See also question G7A02.

G6A13 **What type of component is a thermistor?**

  A. A resistor that is resistant to changes in value with temperature variations
  B. A device having a controlled change in resistance with temperature variations
  C. A special type of transistor for use at very cold temperatures
  D. A capacitor that changes value with temperature

B All resistors change value to some degree with temperature. A thermistor is a special type of resistor whose change in value with temperature is precisely controlled so that it can be used as a temperature sensor.

G6B Rectifiers; solid state diodes and transistors; solar cells; vacuum tubes; batteries

G6B01 **What is the peak-inverse-voltage rating of a rectifier?**

  A. The maximum voltage the rectifier will handle in the conducting direction
  B. 1.4 times the AC frequency
  C. The maximum voltage the rectifier will handle in the non-conducting direction
  D. 2.8 times the AC frequency

C Power-supply rectifier diodes are made from semiconductor material. Diodes allow current to flow only in one direction. If the voltage is high enough, however, current can be forced to flow in the opposite direction, often destroying the diode. The peak inverse voltage rating (PIV) of a rectifier diode is the maximum reverse voltage that should ever be applied to the diode — it is guaranteed to withstand that voltage.

G6B02 **What are the two major ratings that must not be exceeded for silicon-diode rectifiers?**

  A. Peak inverse voltage; average forward current
  B. Average power; average voltage
  C. Capacitive reactance; avalanche voltage
  D. Peak load impedance; peak voltage

A Peak inverse voltage and average forward current are two major ratings that must not be exceeded for silicon diode rectifiers. Peak inverse voltage rating, PIV, is described in question G6B01. The maximum average forward current is the other major rating that must not be exceeded. Forward current causes power to be dissipated in the diode because of the forward voltage drop (0.7 volt in silicon rectifiers). The amount of power is 0.7 V × the average forward current. Too much current overheats and destroys the diode.

G6B03   What is the approximate junction threshold voltage of a germanium diode?

A. 0.1 volt
B. 0.3 volts
C. 0.7 volts
D. 1.0 volts

B   The junction threshold voltage is the voltage at which a diode begins to conduct significant current across its PN junction. The amount of voltage depends on the material from which the diode is constructed. The junction threshold voltage of silicon diodes is approximately 0.7 V and for germanium diodes approximately 0.3 V.

G6B04   When two or more diodes are connected in parallel to increase current handling capacity, what is the purpose of the resistor connected in series with each diode?

A. The resistors ensure the thermal stability of the power supply
B. The resistors regulate the power supply output voltage
C. The resistors ensure that one diode doesn't carry most of the current
D. The resistors act as swamping resistors in the circuit

C   Two or more diodes are sometimes connected in parallel to increase the current-handling ability of a circuit. There should always be a small resistor connected in series with each parallel diode. Without a resistor in series with each diode, one diode may take most of the current because of small variations in threshold voltage, and that could destroy the diode by exceeding its average forward current rating. The resistor value should be chosen to provide a few tenths of a volt drop at the expected forward current.

ARRL0088

Figure G6-5 — Use equalizing resistors when you connect diodes in parallel to increase the forward current-handling capability. The resistor value is chosen to provide a few tenths of a volt drop at the expected forward current.

G6B05   What is the approximate junction threshold voltage of a
            silicon diode?

   A. 0.1 volt
   B. 0.3 volts
   C. 0.7 volts
   D. 1.0 volts

C   See the discussion for question G6B03.

G6B06   Which of the following is an advantage of using a Schottky
            diode in an RF switching circuit as compared to a standard
            silicon diode?

   A. Lower capacitance
   B. Lower inductance
   C. Longer switching times
   D. Higher breakdown voltage

A   The construction of a Schottky diode results in much lower capacitance from
the cathode to the anode. This makes the diode respond better to high-frequency
signals that might be found in a switching power supply or in an RF circuit.

G6B07   What are the stable operating points for a bipolar transistor
            that is used as a switch in a logic circuit?

   A. Its saturation and cut-off regions
   B. Its active region (between cut-off and saturation regions)
   C. Between its peak and valley current points
   D. Between its enhancement and depletion modes

A   When a bipolar transistor is used as a switch in a logic circuit, it is important
that the switch either be "all the way on" or "all the way off." This is achieved
by operating the transistor either in its saturation region to turn the switch on, or
in its cut-off region to turn the switch off.

G6B08   Why is it often necessary to insulate the case of a large power
            transistor?

   A. To increase the beta of the transistor
   B. To improve the power dissipation capability
   C. To reduce stray capacitance
   D. To avoid shorting the collector or drain voltage to ground

D   On some power transistors, the collector or drain is connected to the case to
improve the transfer of heat away from the semiconductor material. This helps
keep the transistor from overheating when controlling high currents, but requires
that the case of the transistor, the collector or drain lead, be insulated from ground
since most circuits do not ground the collector or drain.

G6B09 Which of the following describes the construction of a MOSFET?

A. The gate is formed by a back-biased junction
B. The gate is separated from the channel with a thin insulating layer
C. The source is separated from the drain by a thin insulating later
D. The source is formed by depositing metal on silicon

B A MOSFET (Metal Oxide Semiconductor Field Effect Transistor) is similar to a JFET (Junction Field Effect Transistor), but instead of the gate electrode being in direct contact with the channel between drain and source, it is insulated by a thin insulating layer of oxide. The gate voltage still controls electron flow between the drain and source, but very little current flows in the gate circuit.

G6B10 Which element of a triode vacuum tube is used to regulate the flow of electrons between cathode and plate?

A. Control grid
B. Heater
C. Screen Grid
D. Suppressor grid

A The control grid is closest to the cathode, the element of the tube that generates the electrons. By varying the control grid voltage with respect to the cathode voltage, electron flow between cathode and plate can be controlled.

G6B11 Which of the following solid state devices is most like a vacuum tube in its general characteristics?

A. A bipolar transistor
B. An FET
C. A tunnel diode
D. A varistor

B An FET acts very much like a vacuum tube with the gate electrode taking the role of the control grid, controlling electron flow between the drain and source. The drain corresponds to the plate and the source corresponds to the cathode.

G6B12 What is the primary purpose of a screen grid in a vacuum tube?

A. To reduce grid-to-plate capacitance
B. To increase efficiency
C. To increase the high frequency response
D. To decrease plate resistance

A The screen grid is placed between the plate and control grid and kept at a constant voltage. This isolates the control grid from the plate and reduces the capacitance between them.

G6B13 What is an advantage of the low internal resistance of Nickel Cadmium batteries?

A. Long life
B. High discharge current
C. High voltage
D. Rapid recharge

B Nickel Cadmium (NiCd) batteries are constructed so that they can supply large quantities of current very quickly. This makes them useful in portable power tools and radio transceivers.

G6B14 What is the minimum allowable discharge voltage for maximum life of a standard 12 volt lead acid battery?

A. 6 volts
B. 8.5 volts
C. 10.5 volts
D. 12 volts

C Standard 12 volt lead-acid batteries are composed of six 2 volt cells connected in series. Each cell should not be discharged below 1.75 volts to avoid causing irreversible chemical changes that damage the cell. Thus, the minimum voltage for a standard 12 volt battery is $6 \times 1.75 = 10.5$ volts.

G6B15 When is it acceptable to recharge a carbon-zinc primary cell?

A. As long as the voltage has not been allowed to drop below 1.0 volt
B. When the cell is kept warm during the recharging period
C. When a constant current charger is used
D. Never

D Carbon-zinc batteries are not rechargeable because the chemical reaction that powers them cannot be reversed. Do not attempt to recharge them! If current is forced back through the cell, the resulting chemical reaction releases acid and heat that may breach the battery's case, damaging whatever houses the battery.

G6B16 Which of the following is a rechargeable battery?

A. Carbon-zinc
B. Silver oxide
C. Nickel Metal Hydride
D. Mercury

C Nickel metal hydride (NiMH) batteries are the only rechargeable battery type in this list. Rechargeable batteries are made from chemicals whose current-supplying reaction can be reversed.

G6C Analog and digital integrated circuits (IC's); microprocessors; memory; I/O devices; microwave IC's (MMIC's); display devices

G6C01   Which of the following is most often provided as an analog integrated circuit?

- A. NAND Gate
- B. Gallium Arsenide UHF Receiver "front end" Amplifier
- C. Frequency Counter
- D. Linear voltage regulator

D   A linear voltage regulator is composed of a transistor, a voltage reference diode and an amplifier that compares the circuit output voltage to the voltage reference. The regulator continuously varies the transistor current to keep the output voltage constant. Operation over a continuous range of voltages and currents is what analog integrated circuits do.

G6C02   Which of the following is the most commonly used digital logic family of integrated circuits?

- A. RTL
- B. TTL
- C. CMOS
- D. PMOS

C   CMOS is used in all computers and most consumer electronics, making it the most popular family of digital logic circuits by far.

G6C03   Which of the following is an advantage of CMOS Logic integrated circuits compared to TTL logic circuits?

- A. Low power consumption
- B. High power handling capability
- C. Better suited for RF amplification
- D. Better suited for power supply regulation

A   CMOS circuits consume very little current when operating, only drawing significant power when switching between ON and OFF states.

G6C04   What is meant by the term ROM?

- A. Resistor Operated Memory
- B. Read Only Memory
- C. Random Operational Memory
- D. Resistant to Overload Memory

B   ROM, or read only memory, contains data or program instructions that do not need to be changed. ROM is used to prevent unauthorized changes and because it is often less expensive than other types of data storage.

G6C05 What is meant when memory is characterized as "non-volatile"?

A. It is resistant to radiation damage
B. It is resistant to high temperatures
C. The stored information is maintained even if power is removed
D. The stored information cannot be changed once written

C Non-volatile memory can retain the stored data even if power is removed and restored. It never needs to have the data "refreshed." Volatile memory loses the data if power is removed and often needs to have the data refreshed while in operation, such as for dynamic types of memory.

G6C06 Which type of integrated circuit is an operational amplifier?

A. Digital
B. MMIC
C. Programmable
D. Analog

D An operational amplifier, or op amp, is an analog circuit, operating on a continuous range of voltage and current.

G6C07 What is one disadvantage of an incandescent indicator compared to a LED?

A. Low power consumption
B. High speed
C. Long life
D. High power consumption

D Incandescent indicators (lamps) are bright, but they waste most of the energy supplied to them as heat. For the same amount of light output, LEDs are much more power efficient than incandescent lamps.

G6C08 How is an LED biased when emitting light?

A. Beyond cutoff
B. At the Zener voltage
C. Reverse Biased
D. Forward Biased

D An LED emits light when forward biased so that current flows through the PN junction of the diode. The light is given off when the electrons from the N-type material combine with the holes in the P-type material.

G6C09 Which of the following is a characteristic of a liquid crystal display?

A. It requires ambient or back lighting
B. It offers a wide dynamic range
C. It has a wide viewing angle
D. All of these choices are correct

A A liquid crystal display (LCD) works by blocking the transmission of light through an otherwise transparent layer of liquid crystals. Transparent electrodes are printed on the glass layers on either side of the liquid crystals to form the pattern of the digits, characters, and symbols. When voltage of the right polarity is applied between the electrodes, the liquid crystals twist into a pattern that blocks light. This is why in order to see the desired pattern, an LCD requires ambient light to reflect off the back of the display or an active source of light behind the liquid crystals (backlighting).

G6C10 What is meant by the term MMIC?

A. Multi Megabyte Integrated Circuit
B. Monolithic Microwave Integrated Circuit
C. Military-specification Manufactured Integrated Circuit
D. Mode Modulated Integrated Circuit

B An MMIC is a special type of analog IC containing circuits to perform RF operations such as amplification, modulation and demodulation, and mixing at HF through microwave frequencies. Some MMICs combine several functions, acting as an entire receiver front end, for example. The MMIC is what enables communications engineers to construct low-cost, hand-held mobile phones and GPS receivers, among other sophisticated examples of wireless technology.

G6C11 What is a microprocessor?

A. A low powered analog signal processor used as a microwave detector
B. A miniature computer on a single integrated circuit chip
C. A microwave detector, amplifier, and local oscillator on a chip
D. A low voltage amplifier used in a microwave transmitter modulator stage

B Microprocessors were invented in the early 1970s to take advantage of rapid advances in digital circuit miniaturization. These miniature computers on a single IC consist of arrays of digital gates and logic elements that can retrieve program instructions (known as machine language) and execute the instructions on digital data. Simple microprocessors may be little more than a set of registers that store and exchange data for the program instructions. Complex microprocessors may contain sub-processors that are dedicated to special functions or sophisticated communications interfaces. Some include analog-to-digital converters to provide an all-in-one DSP platform.

G6C12 **What two devices in an amateur radio station might be connected using a USB interface?**

A. Computer and transceiver
B. Microphone and transceiver
C. Amplifier and antenna
D. Power supply and amplifier

A   A USB (Universal Serial Bus) interface is a means of exchanging digital data in a serial stream (meaning one bit at a time). The only pair of devices in the list that have a need to communicate over such an interface are the computer and transceiver.

Practical Circuits

Your General class exam (Element 3) will consist of 35 questions taken from the General class question pool as prepared by the Volunteer Examiner Coordinators' Question Pool Committee. A certain number of questions are taken from each of the 10 subelements. There will be 2 questions from the subelement shown in this chapter. These questions are divided into 2 groups, labeled G7A and G7B.

G7A Power supplies; transmitters and receivers; filters; schematic drawing symbols

G7A01 What safety feature does a power-supply bleeder resistor provide?

A. It acts as a fuse for excess voltage
B. It discharges the filter capacitors
C. It removes shock hazards from the induction coils
D. It eliminates ground-loop current

B A bleeder resistor is installed across a filter capacitor to discharge the capacitor when power is not supplied to the circuit. This is to minimize the risk of electrical shock from a charge stored in the filter capacitor if the supply enclosure is opened, exposing the capacitor terminals.

Figure G7-1 — A bleeder resistor is a safety feature that discharges a power supply filter capacitor when the supply is turned off.

G7A02 What components are used in a power-supply filter network?

    A. Diodes

    B. Transformers and transistors

    C. Quartz crystals

    D. Capacitors and inductors

D   A power supply filter network consists of capacitors and inductors used to smooth out the voltage pulses from the rectifier output. Capacitors oppose changes in voltage while the inductors oppose changes in current. The combination results in a constant dc output voltage from the supply.

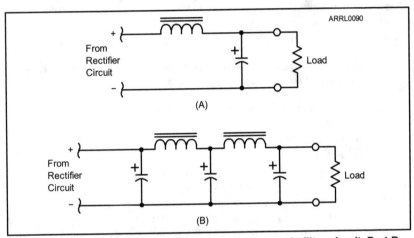

Figure G7-2 — Part A shows a choke-input power-supply filter circuit. Part B shows a capacitor-input, multisection filter.

G7A03 **What should be the minimum peak-inverse-voltage rating of the rectifier in a full-wave power supply?**

    A. One-quarter the normal output voltage of the power supply

    B. Half the normal output voltage of the power supply

    C. Double the normal peak output voltage of the power supply

    D. Equal to the normal output voltage of the power supply

C   Rectifier diodes allow current to flow only in the forward direction. If the voltage is strong enough in the reverse direction, however, current can be forced back through the diode, often destroying it. The voltage required to make this happen is the peak inverse voltage (PIV). The PIV rating of the rectifiers in a full-wave power supply should be at least twice the normal peak output voltage of the power supply.

G7A04 **What should be the approximate minimum peak-inverse-voltage rating of the rectifier in a half-wave power supply?**

A. One-half the normal peak output voltage of the power supply
B. Half the normal output voltage of the power supply
C. Equal to the normal output voltage of the power supply
D. Two times the normal peak output voltage of the power supply

D The PIV rating of the rectifiers in a half-wave power supply should be at least twice the normal peak output voltage of the power supply. (See also the discussion for question G7A03.)

G7A05 **What should be the impedance of a low-pass filter as compared to the impedance of the transmission line into which it is inserted?**

A. Substantially higher
B. About the same
C. Substantially lower
D. Twice the transmission line impedance

B To prevent unwanted reflected power and elevated SWR, keep all elements of the feed line and antenna system at the same impedance. A low-pass filter, designed to be installed at the transmitter output, should have the same impedance as the transmission line.

G7A06 Which of the following might be used to process signals from the balanced modulator and send them to the mixer in a single-sideband phone transmitter?

A. Carrier oscillator
B. Filter
C. IF amplifier
D. RF amplifier

B In a single-sideband transmitter, the modulating audio is added to the RF signal in the balanced modulator. The balanced modulator also balances out or cancels the original carrier signal, leaving a double-sideband, suppressed-carrier signal. A filter then removes one of the sidebands, leaving a single-sideband signal that is sent to the mixer. In the mixer it combines with the signal from a local oscillator (LO) to produce the RF signal that is amplified and sent to the antenna. The LO shown in Figure G7-3 is crystal-controlled for fixed-frequency operation. Replacing the crystal-controlled LO with a variable-frequency oscillator (VFO) results in a tunable transmitter similar to those in most modern transceivers.

G7A07 Which circuit is used to combine signals from the carrier oscillator and speech amplifier and send the result to the filter in a typical single-sideband phone transmitter?

A. Mixer
B. Detector
C. IF amplifier
D. Balanced modulator

D See the discussion for question G7A06 and Figure G7-3.

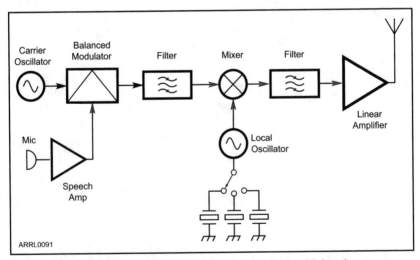

Figure G7-3 — This block diagram shows a basic single-sideband, suppressed-carrier (SSB) transmitter.

G7A08 **What circuit is used to process signals from the RF amplifier and local oscillator and send the result to the IF filter in a superheterodyne receiver**

A. Balanced modulator
B. IF amplifier
C. Mixer
D. Detector

C   In a superheterodyne receiver, the mixer combines signals from the RF amplifier and the local oscillator (LO) and sends those signals to the IF filter. The IF filter passes the desired range of frequencies while rejecting the signals at higher and lower frequencies.

G7A09 **What circuit is used to process signals from the IF amplifier and the BFO and send the result to the AF amplifier in a single-sideband phone superheterodyne receiver?**

A. RF oscillator
B. IF filter
C. Balanced modulator
D. Product detector

D   In a superheterodyne receiver, the product detector circuit recovers the modulating audio signal by combining the output of the intermediate frequency (IF) amplifier and the beat frequency oscillator (BFO). The recovered audio signal is then passed to the audio frequency (AF) amplifier. (See also the discussion for question G7A08 and Figure G7-4.)

Figure G7-4 — This block diagram shows a simple superheterodyne SSB receiver.

G7A10   What is an advantage of a crystal controlled transmitter?

    A. Stable output frequency
    B. Excellent modulation clarity
    C. Ease of switching between bands
    D. Ease of changing frequency

A   Using a crystal to control the frequency of an oscillator results in a very precise and stable output signal. Crystals only operate on a single frequency and must be changed if the oscillator's frequency is to be changed.

G7A11   What is the simplest combination of stages that can be combined to implement a superheterodyne receiver?

    A. RF amplifier, detector, audio amplifier
    B. RF amplifier, mixer, if amplifier
    C. HF oscillator, mixer, detector
    D. HF oscillator, product detector, audio amplifier

C   By definition, a superheterodyne receiver must contain a mixer and a local oscillator. One additional stage, a detector, is necessary to recover the modulating audio. Thus, the simplest superheterodyne consists of a mixer, oscillator and detector. Practical receivers add more amplifiers to improve sensitivity and filters to reject unwanted signals.

G7A12   What type of receiver is suitable for CW and SSB reception but does not require a mixer stage or an IF amplifier?

    A. A super-regenerative receiver
    B. A TRF receiver
    C. A super-heterodyne receiver
    D. A direct conversion receiver

D   A direct-conversion receiver is essentially a product detector that converts incoming signals directly from RF to audio. The receiver's gain is supplied entirely by the AF amplifier stage.

G7A13 What type of circuit is used in many FM receivers to convert signals coming from the IF amplifier to audio?

A. Product detector
B. Phase inverter
C. Mixer
D. Discriminator

D A frequency discriminator converts the variations in frequency of the limiter's output signal into amplitude variations, recovering the modulating audio signal. A quadrature detector is another type of FM demodulation circuit that converts changes in frequency into amplitude variations.

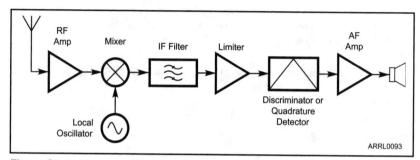

Figure G7-5 — This block diagram shows a simple FM receiver.

G7A14 Which of the following is a desirable characteristic for capacitors used to filter the DC output of a switching power supply?

A. Low equivalent series resistance
B. High equivalent series resistance
C. Low Temperature coefficient
D. High Temperature coefficient

A It is important to use filter capacitors that have a low equivalent series resistance (ESR) rating for the output filter of a switching power supply. Low ESR means that currents flowing into and out of the capacitor as it smoothes the output voltage will not cause voltage variations.

G7A15 Which of the following is an advantage of a switched-mode power supply as compared to a linear power supply?

A. Faster switching time makes higher output voltage possible
B. Fewer circuit components are required
C. High frequency operation allows the use of smaller components
D. All of these choices are correct

C   Switched-mode power supplies use an oscillator operating at a frequency much higher than the 60 Hz ac line current. (Oscillator frequencies of 50 kHz or more are commonly used.) This allows the use of small, lightweight transformers. While the transformer in a linear power supply capable of supplying 20 amperes might weigh 15 or 20 pounds, the transformer for a switched-mode power supply with a similar current rating might only weigh 1 or 2 pounds (or less)! Switched-mode power supplies have more complex circuits than linear supplies and generally require more components than a simple linear supply.

G7A16 What portion of the AC cycle is converted to DC by a half-wave rectifier?

A. 90 degrees
B. 180 degrees
C. 270 degrees
D. 360 degrees

B   Since there are 360 degrees in a full cycle of ac, a half-wave rectifier converts 180 degrees of the ac input waveform to dc.

Figure G7-6 — This circuit is a basic half-wave rectifier circuit, with a load resistor but no filter. The waveform shown at the right represents the output voltage and diode current. The values of the peak output voltage, average output voltage and peak inverse voltage across the diodes are listed.

G7A17　**What portion of the AC cycle is converted to DC by a full-wave rectifier?**

A. 90 degrees
B. 180 degrees
C. 270 degrees
D. 360 degrees

D　Since there are 360 degrees in a full cycle of ac, a full-wave rectifier converts 360 degrees of the ac input waveform to dc.

G7A18　**What is the output waveform of an unfiltered full-wave rectifier connected to a resistive load?**

A. A series of DC pulses at twice the frequency of the AC input
B. A series of DC pulses at the same frequency as the AC input
C. A sine wave at half the frequency of the AC input
D. A steady DC voltage

A　A full-wave rectifier changes alternating current with positive and negative half cycles into a fluctuating current with all positive pulses. Since the current in this case has not yet been filtered, it is a series of pulses at twice the frequency of the ac input.

Figure G7-7 — This circuit shows a simple full-wave rectifier with a load resistor but no filter. The waveform shown at the right represents the output voltage and diode current. The values of the peak output voltage, average output voltage and peak inverse voltage across the diodes are listed.

Question Pool Figure G7-1 — Refer to this figure for questions G7A19 through G7A24.

Question Pool Figure G7-1

G7A19 Which symbol in figure G7-1 represents a fixed resistor?

A. Symbol 2
B. Symbol 6
C. Symbol 3
D. Symbol 12

C Symbol 3 represents a fixed resistor.

G7A20 Which symbol in figure G7-1 represents a single cell battery?

A. Symbol 5
B. Symbol 12
C. Symbol 8
D. Symbol 13

D Symbol 13 represents a single battery cell. The longer line is the positive terminal. Batteries consisting of more than one cell repeat the sequence of longer and shorter lines.

G7A21   Which symbol in figure G7-1 represents a NPN transistor?

A.   Symbol 2
B.   Symbol 4
C.   Symbol 10
D.   Symbol 12

B   Symbol 4 represents an NPN transistor because the arrowhead from emitter to base points towards the base connection. A mnemonic to remember the arrow's direction is "NPN — No Pointing In" and "PNP — Point In Please."

G7A22   Which symbol in figure G7-1 represents a variable capacitor?

A.   Symbol 2
B.   Symbol 11
C.   Symbol 5
D.   Symbol 12

C   The arrow on Symbol 5 indicates that the capacitor's value is variable.

G7A23   Which symbol in figure G7-1 represents a transformer?

A.   Symbol 6
B.   Symbol 4
C.   Symbol 10
D.   Symbol 2

A   Two inductors, one on either side of the double lines indicating a magnetic core, form the transformer represented by Symbol 6.

G7A24   Which symbol in figure G7-1 represents a single pole switch?

A.   Symbol 2
B.   Symbol 3
C.   Symbol 11
D.   Symbol 12

C   Symbol 11 represents a single-pole switch. The circles represent the switch's contacts and the straight line the mechanism that connects them. The switch is shown in the OPEN position.

G7B Digital circuits (gates, flip-flops, shift registers); amplifiers and oscillators

G7B01   Which of the following describes a "flip-flop" circuit?

A. A transmit-receive circuit

B. A digital circuit with two stable states

C. An RF limiter

D. A voice-operated switch

B   A flip-flop circuit changes its output between one of two stable states ("0" and "1") with each instance of an input signal, such as a pulse or change in input state.

G7B02   Why do digital circuits use the binary number system?

A. Binary "ones" and "zeros" are easy to represent with an "on" or "off" state

B. The binary number system is most accurate

C. Binary numbers are more compatible with analog circuitry

D. All of these answers are correct

A   Binary numbers are easily represented by circuits that have two stable states — ON and OFF. The states can be used to represent either a binary 0 or 1 as the designer chooses.

G7B03 What is the output of a two-input NAND gate, given both inputs are "one"?

- A. Two
- B. One
- C. Zero
- D. Minus One

C A NAND (NOT-AND) gate consists of an AND gate with its output inverted. If both inputs to a NAND gate are true or "1", the AND function is also "1", which is then inverted to "0" as shown in Figure G7-8D.

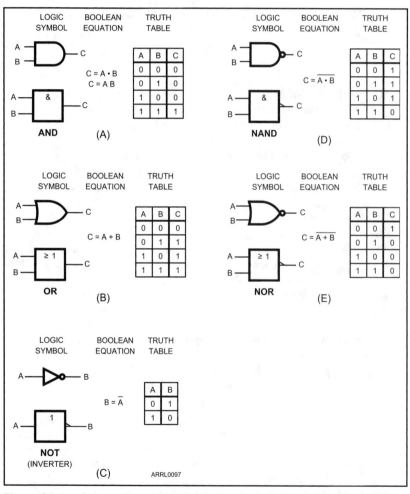

Figure G7-8 — Schematic symbols for the basic digital logic functions with the logic equations and truth tables that describe their operation. A two-input AND gate is shown at A, a two-input OR gate at B, an inverter at C, a two-input NAND gate at D and a two-input NOR gate at E.

G7B04 What is the output of a NOR gate given that both inputs are "zero"?

A. Zero
B. One
C. Minus one
D. The opposite from the previous state

B A NOR (NOT-OR) gate consists of an OR gate with its output inverted. If both inputs to a NOR gate are false or "0", the OR function is also "0", which is then inverted to "1". (See also the discussion for question G7B03 and Figure G7-8E.)

G7B05 How many states are there in a 3-bit binary counter?

A. 3
B. 6
C. 8
D. 16

C There are 8 states because the number of states in a binary counter is 2^N, where N is the number of bits in the counter. A 2-bit counter has $2^2 = 4$ states, a 3-bit counter $2^3 = 8$ states, a 4-bit counter $2^4 = 16$ states, and so forth.

G7B06 What is a shift register?

A. An clocked array of circuits that passes data in steps along the array
B. An array of operational amplifiers used for tri-state arithmetic operations
C. A digital mixer
D. An analog mixer

A A shift register consists of a sequence of flip-flop circuits connected output-to-input and sharing a common clock input signal. With each pulse of the clock signal, the input signal of the shift register is transferred to the output of the first flip-flop and each subsequent flip-flop's output is passed to the next flip-flop's input.

G7B07 What are the basic components of virtually all oscillators?

A. An amplifier and a divider
B. A frequency multiplier and a mixer
C. A circulator and a filter operating in a feed-forward loop
D. A filter and an amplifier operating in a feedback loop

D To make an oscillator requires an amplifier and a circuit that routes some of the amplifier's output signal back to the input (called a "feedback loop") such that it is reinforced in the amplifier output. This is called positive feedback. A filter in the feedback loop is used so only signals at the desired frequency are reinforced. Starting with random noise, the oscillator gradually builds up an output signal at the filter frequency until it is self-sustaining.

G7B08 What determines the frequency of an RC oscillator?

A. The ratio of the capacitors in the feedback loop
B. The value of the inductor in the tank circuit
C. The phase shift of the RC feedback circuit
D. The gain of the amplifier

C (See also the discussion for question G7B07.) The feedback loop in an RC oscillator is made from RC (resistor-capacitor) circuits that shift the phase of the signal fed back to the input. The RC oscillator's output is at the frequency at which the RC circuit's phase shift is 180 degrees. The amplifier in an RC oscillator inverts the input signal, adding another 180 degrees of phase shift, so the oscillations are self-sustaining.

G7B09 What determines the frequency of an LC oscillator?

A. The number of stages in the counter
B. The number of stages in the divider
C. The inductance and capacitance in the tank circuit
D. The time delay of the lag circuit

C An LC oscillator uses a parallel LC circuit (a tank circuit) as the filter in the feedback loop. (See also the discussion for question G7B07.)

G7B10 Which of the following is a characteristic of a Class A amplifier?

A. Low standby power
B. High Efficiency
C. No need for bias
D. Low distortion

D Class A amplifiers are used when low distortion is required. Class A means that current flows in the amplifying device — whether a transistor or vacuum tube — at all times. Because the amplifier is never saturated or cut off, its operation can be optimized for linear reproduction of the input signal. The tradeoff is that Class A amplifiers consume power 100% of the time, require a source of bias to keep them on in the absence of an input signal, and aren't particularly efficient.

G7B11 **For which of the following modes is a Class C power stage appropriate for amplifying a modulated signal?**

A. SSB
B. CW
C. AM
D. All of these answers are correct

B   A Class C amplifier conducts current during less than half of the input signal cycle, resulting in high distortion. This rules out Class C amplifiers for any form of amplitude-modulation, such as SSB or AM. Class C amplifiers can be used for CW since that mode requires only the presence or absence of a signal. Similarly, Class C is suitable for FM signals that only depend on signal frequency, which is not changed by the amplifier. Class C amplifiers generate significant harmonics, so they require filtering for use as transmitter outputs.

G7B12 **Which of the following is an advantage of a Class C amplifier?**

A. High efficiency
B. Linear operation
C. No need for tuned circuits
D. All of these answers are correct

A   Class C amplifiers act a lot like switches — they turn on for a fraction of the input signal's cycle and stay off the rest of the time. While these amplifiers are not linear at all and require filters to eliminate the harmonics in their output, they are quite efficient.

G7B13 **How is the efficiency of an RF power amplifier determined?**

A. Divide the DC input power by the DC output power
B. Divide the RF output power by the DC input power
C. Multiply the RF input power by the reciprocal of the RF output power
D. Add the RF input power to the DC output power

B   Efficiency is defined as the total output power divided by the total input power and is measured in percent. For an RF amplifier, total output power is measured by a wattmeter. The total input power is the dc power required for the amplifier to operate. For example, if to produce 1200 watts of RF output the amplifier requires 1000 mA of plate current at a voltage of 2000 V:

$$\text{Efficiency} = \frac{1200 \text{ watts}}{1 \text{ A} \times 2000 \text{ V}} = \frac{1200}{2000} = 60\%$$

G7B14 **Which of the following describes a linear amplifier?**

    A. Any RF power amplifier used in conjunction with an amateur transceiver

    B. An amplifier whose output preserves the input waveform

    C. A Class C high efficiency amplifier

    D. An amplifier used as a frequency multiplier

B   A linear amplifier is defined as one whose output waveform is a copy of the input waveform, although larger in amplitude. Hams refer to power amplifiers as "linears," whether they are operating linearly (for AM or SSB modes) or not (for CW or FM). It is important to understand that an amplifier designed for FM will not be suitable as an SSB amplifier because it is not linear.

Signals and Emissions

Your General class exam (Element 3) will consist of 35 questions taken from the General class question pool as prepared by the Volunteer Examiner Coordinators' Question Pool Committee. A certain number of questions are taken from each of the 10 subelements. There will be 2 questions from the subelement shown in this chapter. These questions are divided into 2 groups, labeled G8A and G8B.

G8A Carriers and modulation: AM; FM; single and double sideband; modulation envelope; deviation; overmodulation

G8A01 What is the name of the process that changes the envelope of an RF wave to convey information?

A. Phase modulation
B. Frequency modulation
C. Spread Spectrum modulation
D. Amplitude modulation

D There are several ways to change or modulate an RF wave for the purpose of conveying information. CW simply turns the signal on and off to convey information. Amplitude modulation changes the strength or amplitude of the wave, and frequency modulation changes its frequency. Phase modulation conveys information by changing the phase of the wave.

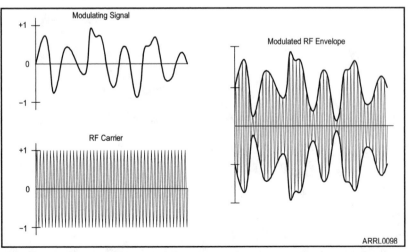

Figure G8-1 — This drawing shows the relationship between the modulating audio waveform, the RF carrier and the resulting RF envelope in a double-sideband, full-carrier amplitude-modulated signal.

G8A02 What is the name of the process that changes the phase angle of an RF wave to convey information?

A. Phase convolution
B. Phase modulation
C. Angle convolution
D. Radian Inversion

B See the discussion for question G8A01.

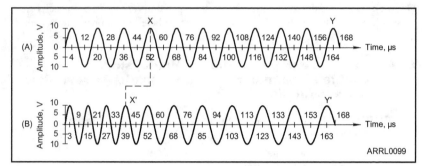

Figure G8-2 — This drawing shows a graphical representation of phase modulation. The unmodulated wave is shown at A. Part B shows the modulated wave. After modulation, cycle X′ occurs earlier than cycle X did. All the cycles to the left of X′ are compressed, and to the right they are spread out.

G8A03 What is the name of the process which changes the frequency of an RF wave to convey information?

A. Frequency convolution
B. Frequency transformation
C. Frequency conversion
D. Frequency modulation

D See the discussion for question G8A01.

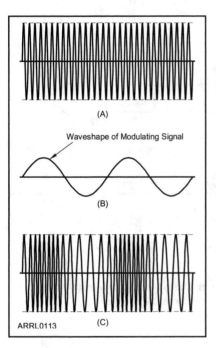

(A)

Waveshape of Modulating Signal

(B)

(C)

ARRL0113

Figure G8-3 — This drawing shows a graphical representation of frequency modulation. In the unmodulated carrier at Part A, each RF cycle takes the same amount of time to complete. When the modulating signal of Part B is applied, the carrier frequency is increased or decreased according to the amplitude and polarity of the modulating signal. Part C shows the modulated RF wave.

G8A04   **What emission is produced by a reactance modulator connected to an RF power amplifier?**

A. Multiplex modulation
B. Phase modulation
C. Amplitude modulation
D. Pulse modulation

B   Reactance modulators are the most common method of generating phase modulation (PM) signals. Phase modulators cause the output signal phase to vary with both the modulating signal's amplitude and frequency. (See also the discussion for question G8A01.)

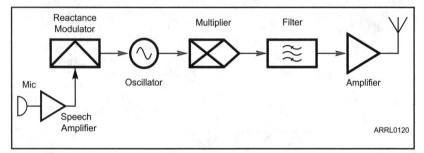

Figure G8-4 — This block diagram shows a phase-modulated transmitter, which uses a reactance modulator. The transmitted signal can be received by the same receiver as an FM signal.

G8A05   **What type of transmission varies the instantaneous power level of the RF signal to convey information?**

A. Frequency shift keying
B. Pulse modulation
C. Frequency modulation
D. Amplitude modulation

D   In an AM transmission, at any given instant the amplitude or envelope of the RF signal changes according to the modulating audio signal. (See also the discussion for question G8A01 and Figure G8-1.)

G8A06 **What is one advantage of carrier suppression in a single-sideband phone transmission?**

A. Audio fidelity is improved
B. Greater modulation percentage is obtainable with lower distortion
C. More transmitter power can be put into the remaining sideband
D. Simpler receiving equipment can be used

C In a single-sideband, suppressed-carrier, amplitude-modulated transmitter, the RF carrier signal is reduced or suppressed. The less energy that is used by the carrier, the more power that can be put into the sidebands. This increases the efficiency of the system.

Figure G8-5 — This drawing shows the frequency spectrum of an amplitude-modulated radio signal. Part A shows a double-sideband, full-carrier signal. When the carrier is removed, only the two sidebands are left, as shown in Part B. When one sideband is suppressed, as shown in Part C, the full transmitter power can be concentrated in one sideband.

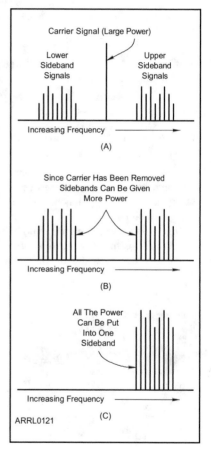

G8A07 Which of the following phone emissions uses the narrowest frequency bandwidth?

    A. Single sideband
    B. Double sideband
    C. Phase modulation
    D. Frequency modulation

A   In a single-sideband (SSB) amplitude-modulated transmitter, the RF carrier signal is reduced or suppressed, and one of the sidebands is removed. Suppression of the carrier allows more power to be put into the sideband. Because the carrier is suppressed and one sideband is filtered out, only enough frequency bandwidth is required to transmit a single sideband. This has the narrowest bandwidth of all the popular phone emissions. The bandwidth of an SSB signal is between about 2 and 3 kHz, the bandwidth of a double-sideband AM signal is about 6 kHz and the bandwidth of frequency and phase modulated phone signals is about 16 kHz.

G8A08   What happens to the signal of an over-modulated single-sideband phone transmitter?

    A. It becomes louder with no other effects
    B. It occupies less bandwidth with poor high frequency response
    C. It has higher fidelity and improved signal to noise ratio
    D. It becomes distorted and occupies more bandwidth

D   When a signal is overmodulated the envelope becomes distorted, making it difficult to understand. This can also cause splatter — a signal with excessive bandwidth that results in interference to nearby signals. Overmodulation is caused by having the microphone gain control set too high or by overprocessing the signal with a speech processor. For proper adjustment on most transmitters, the microphone gain control should be adjusted so that there is a slight movement of the ALC meter on modulation peaks. An overmodulated signal is shown on an oscilloscope with flattening at the maximum levels of the envelope. This is referred to as flattopping.

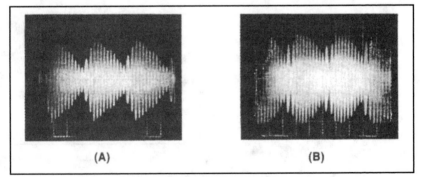

Figure G8-6 — Part A shows the waveform of a properly adjusted SSB transmitter. Part B shows a severely clipped, distorted signal.

G8A09 What control is typically adjusted for proper ALC setting on an amateur single sideband transceiver?

A. The RF Clipping Level
B. Audio or microphone gain
C. Antenna inductance or capacitance
D. Attenuator Level

B To reduce overmodulation, the automatic level control (ALC) circuit reduces microphone gain when it detects excessive audio levels. For proper adjustment on most transmitters, the microphone gain control should be adjusted so that there is a slight movement of the ALC meter on modulation peaks. (See also the discussion for question G8A08 and Figure G8-6.)

G8A10 What is meant by flat-topping of a single-sideband phone transmission?

A. Signal distortion caused by insufficient collector current
B. The transmitter's automatic level control is properly adjusted
C. Signal distortion caused by excessive drive
D. The transmitter's carrier is properly suppressed

C Part B of Figure G8-6 with question G8A08 shows an overmodulated SSB signal as seen on an oscilloscope. Note the flattening at the maximum levels of the envelope. This is referred to as flattopping. (See also the discussion for question G8A08.)

G8A11 What happens to the RF carrier signal when a modulating audio signal is applied to an FM transmitter?

A. The carrier frequency changes proportionally to the instantaneous amplitude of the modulating signal
B. The carrier frequency changes proportionally to the amplitude and frequency of the modulating signal
C. The carrier amplitude changes proportionally to the instantaneous frequency of the modulating signal
D. The carrier phase changes proportionally to the instantaneous amplitude of the modulating signal

A Frequency modulation (FM) results when the modulating signal causes the frequency of an oscillator to change in proportion to the modulating signal's amplitude. If the oscillator's frequency changes in proportion to both the modulating signal's amplitude and frequency, the result is phase modulation (PM).

G8A12 What signal(s) would be found at the output of a properly adjusted balanced modulator?

A. Both upper and lower sidebands
B. Either upper or lower sideband, but not both
C. Both upper and lower sidebands and the carrier
D. The modulating signal and the unmodulated carrier

A The process of mixing two ac signals creates two new signals. One of the new signals has a frequency equal to the sum of the two input signal frequencies and the other new signal has a frequency equal to the difference between the two input signal frequencies. The output signal from most mixers will also include some signal energy at the original input frequencies as well. A mixer can generate a double-sideband signal if the input signals are the carrier and the modulating audio.

A balanced modulator is a mixer that includes some additional circuitry that can be adjusted to balance out or cancel the unwanted signals that remain at the carrier and modulating audio frequencies. When a balanced modulator is properly adjusted, neither of the original input signals reach the modulator output, only the sum and difference frequency signals. These signals are the upper (sum) and lower (difference) sidebands of an AM signal. A balanced modulator is used to produce the modulated RF signal for a single-sideband transmitter. The unwanted sideband is removed by a filter to produce the SSB signal.

G8B Frequency mixing; multiplication; HF data communications; bandwidths of various modes

G8B01   What receiver stage combines a 14.250 MHz input signal with a 13.795 MHz oscillator signal to produce a 455 kHz intermediate frequency (IF) signal?

    A. Mixer
    B. BFO
    C. VFO
    D. Multiplier

A   The mixer stage in a receiver combines the input signal with an oscillator signal to produce the sum and the difference of the two signals. Filters or mixer design will give one desired new signal, known as the intermediate frequency (IF) signal. For example, if a 13.795 MHz variable frequency oscillator (VFO) signal is mixed with a 14.25 MHz RF signal, it will produce new signals at 28.045 MHz and 0.455 MHz, or 455 kHz. A low-pass filter will remove the 28.045 MHz signal and pass the 455 kHz IF signal.

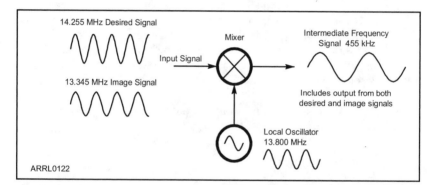

Figure G8-7 — The mixer stage in a receiver combines an RF input signal with a local oscillator (LO) signal to produce an intermediate frequency (IF) signal.

G8B02 If a receiver mixes a 13.800 MHz VFO with a 14.255 MHz received signal to produce a 455 kHz intermediate frequency (IF) signal, what type of interference will a 13.345 MHz signal produce in the receiver?

A. Local oscillator
B. Image response
C. Mixer interference
D. Intermediate interference

B The mixer stage in a receiver combines the input signal with an oscillator signal to produce the sum and the difference of the two signals. Filters or mixer design will select the desired new signal, known as the intermediate frequency (IF) signal. In this case the input signal is 14.255 MHz and the oscillator signal is 13.800 MHz. The sum of these two signals is 28.055 MHz and the difference, which is used as the intermediate frequency, is 0.455 MHz or 455 kHz. These signals are then passed through a filter to eliminate the unwanted frequencies leaving only the desired intermediate frequency of 455 kHz.

A signal at 13.455 MHz, when subtracted from the 13.800 MHz oscillator signal will also produce the 455 kHz intermediate frequency. (See Figure G8-7). When an undesired input signal also produces a signal at the intermediate frequency, the resulting interference is called image response interference. One way to reduce image response interference is to use an input filter that allows signals in the desired receive frequency range to pass through, but blocks signals outside of that range.

G8B03 What stage in a transmitter would change a 5.3 MHz input signal to 14.3 MHz?

A. A mixer
B. A beat frequency oscillator
C. A frequency multiplier
D. A linear translator

A The mixer stage in a transmitter combines the local oscillator (LO) input signal with an RF signal at the intermediate frequency to produce the sum and the difference of the two signals. Filtering the output signal leaves one signal at the desired RF output frequency. For this example, an LO frequency of 9 MHz would give the desired RF output. (9 MHz + 5.3 MHz = 14.3 MHz.) Alternatively, an LO frequency of 19.6 MHz could also be used. (19.6 MHz – 5.3 MHz = 14.3 MHz.) See Figure G8-7 with question G8B01.

G8B04   **What is the name of the stage in a VHF FM transmitter that selects a harmonic of an HF signal to reach the desired operating frequency?**

A. Mixer
B. Reactance modulator
C. Pre-emphasis network
D. Multiplier

D   An FM transmitter often makes use of a device called a frequency multiplier. In a VHF FM transmitter, a reactance modulator operates on a radio-frequency oscillator that is normally operating in the high-frequency (HF) range. A frequency multiplier doubles or triples the frequency of the modulated signal, usually by generating harmonics of the modulated HF signal and selecting one for output to the next stage in the transmitter. Sometimes several multiplier stages are required to produce a signal at the desired output frequency.

G8B05   **Why isn't frequency modulated (FM) phone used below 29.5 MHz?**

A. The transmitter efficiency for this mode is low
B. Harmonics could not be attenuated to practical levels
C. The bandwidth would exceed FCC limits
D. The frequency stability would not be adequate

C   FM phone signals have a bandwidth of about 16 kHz. At frequencies below 29.5 MHz, the maximum FCC allowable bandwidths are narrower than 16 kHz. The HF bands are relatively narrow, and would not be able to accommodate many wide bandwidth FM signals.

G8B06   **What is the total bandwidth of an FM-phone transmission having a 5 kHz deviation and a 3 kHz modulating frequency?**

A. 3 kHz
B. 5 kHz
C. 8 kHz
D. 16 kHz

D   To determine bandwidth of an FM-phone transmission, use the following formula:

$$BW = 2 \times (D + M)$$

where:

BW = bandwidth

D = frequency deviation (the instantaneous change in frequency for a given signal)

M = maximum modulating audio frequency

The total bandwidth of an FM-phone transmission having a 5 kHz deviation and a 3 kHz modulating frequency would be:

$$2 \times (5 \text{ kHz} + 3 \text{ kHz}) = 16 \text{ kHz}$$

G8B07   What is the frequency deviation for a 12.21-MHz reactance-modulated oscillator in a 5-kHz deviation, 146.52-MHz FM-phone transmitter?

A. 101.75 Hz
B. 416.7 Hz
C. 5 kHz
D. 60 kHz

B   An FM transmitter often makes use of a device called a frequency multiplier. In a VHF FM transmitter, a reactance modulator operates on a radio-frequency oscillator that is normally operating in the high-frequency (HF) range. A frequency multiplier doubles or triples the frequency of the modulated signal, usually by generating harmonics of the modulated HF signal and selecting one for output to the next stage in the transmitter. Sometimes several multiplier stages are required to produce a signal at the desired output frequency. When an FM signal's frequency is multiplied, both the carrier frequency and the amount of deviation are multiplied. This is why the deviation of the modulated oscillator is less than that of the final output signal.

To determine the oscillator frequency deviation, divide the output frequency by the oscillator frequency to determine the multiplication factor of the transmitter. Then divide the desired output deviation by the multiplication factor. The frequency deviation for a 12.21 MHz reactance-modulated oscillator in a 5 kHz deviation, 146.52 MHz FM-phone transmitter is 416.7 Hz.

$$\text{Multiplication Factor} = \frac{\text{Transmitter Frequency}}{\text{HF Oscillator Frequency}} = \frac{146.52 \text{ MHz}}{12.21 \text{ MHz}} = 12$$

Then:

$$\text{Desired Oscillator Frequency} = \frac{\text{Transmitter Deviation}}{\text{Multiplication Factor}} = \frac{5000 \text{ Hz}}{12} = 416.7 \text{ Hz}$$

G8B08   How is frequency shift related to keying speed in an FSK signal?

A. The frequency shift in hertz must be at least four times the keying speed in WPM
B. The frequency shift must not exceed 15 Hz per WPM of keying speed
C. Greater keying speeds require greater frequency shifts
D. Greater keying speeds require smaller frequency shifts

C   When high keying speeds are used, the receive demodulator is unable to discern the different output frequencies quickly enough if the two tones of an FSK signal are too close together. As a result, greater keying speeds require greater frequency shifts to allow proper reception.

G8B09 **What do RTTY, Morse code, PSK31 and packet communications have in common?**

A. They require the same bandwidth
B. They are digital modes
C. They use on/off keying
D. They use phase shift modulation

B Baudot RTTY, Morse code, PSK31 and packet radio are all communications methods that use a digital code to transfer information.

G8B10 **When transmitting a data mode signal, why is it important to know the duty cycle of the mode you are using?**

A. To aid in tuning your transmitter
B. To prevent damage to your transmitter's final output stage
C. To allow time for the other station to break in during a transmission
D. All of these choices are correct

B Most Amateur Radio transmitters are not designed to operate at full power output for an extended time. The final output stage is not able to dissipate all of the excess heat that is generated when the transmitter is producing full output power continuously. When you are operating CW, for example, the transmitter is turned on and off to form the Morse code characters so that the transmitter is only operating at full power about 40 to 50% of the time. During the off times, the amplifier stage cools sufficiently to allow full-power operation. When you are operating single-sideband voice, the transmitter is producing full power only when your voice reaches maximum amplitude. For a typical SSB conversation, the transmitter is operating at full power only about 20 to 25% of the time.

When you are operating some data modes, however, your transmitter may be operating at full power the entire time you are transmitting. For Baudot radioteletype the transmitter is producing full output power, switching between the mark and space tones of the code, so the duty cycle is 100%. For PSK31 and similar modes, the transmitter is producing full power for virtually the entire transmit time, so the duty cycle is 100%. PACTOR, packet radio and a few other modes have slightly reduced duty cycles because the transmitter sends some data and then waits to receive an acknowledgement. If you are operating a high-duty-cycle mode you should reduce your transmit power to prevent overheating the amplifier. Reduce your transmitter power to about 50% of maximum output power for most data modes.

G8B11 What part of the 20 meter band is most commonly used for PSK31 operation?

A. At the bottom of the slow-scan TV segment, near 14.230 MHz
B. At the top of the SSB phone segment, near 14.325 MHz
C. In the middle of the CW segment, near 14.100 MHz
D. Below the RTTY segment, near 14.070 MHz

D In order to minimize interference between various modes, amateurs follow an agreement referred to as a band plan. The band plan specifies the location of various emissions on the band. On the 20-meter band, most of the PSK31 activity will be at the low-frequency end of the RTTY segment, near 14.070 MHz. Tune your radio to 14.07015 MHz and use the "waterfall display" of your PSK31 computer program to select signals across the audio passband of your receiver.

G8B12 What is another term for the mixing of two RF signals?

A. Heterodyning
B. Synthesizing
C. Cancellation
D. Multiplying

A The process of mixing signals is sometimes called heterodyning. A receiver that mixes a local oscillator (LO) signal with a received RF signal to produce a signal at some intermediate frequency (IF) that is higher in frequency than the baseband audio signal is called a superheterodyne receiver, or a superhet. The IF signal is processed further by filtering and amplifying it, and then converting the signal to baseband audio. The audio signal is further amplified and fed to a speaker, or it is connected to headphones so you can hear the received signal.

Antennas and Feedlines

Your General class exam (Element 3) will consist of 35 questions taken from the General class question pool as prepared by the Volunteer Examiner Coordinators' Question Pool Committee. A certain number of questions are taken from each of the 10 subelements. There will be 4 questions from the subelement shown in this chapter. These questions are divided into 4 groups, labeled G9A through G9D.

G9A Antenna feedlines: characteristic impedance, and attenuation; SWR calculation, measurement and effects; matching networks

G9A01 Which of the following factors help determine the characteristic impedance of a parallel conductor antenna feedline?

A. The distance between the centers of the conductors and the radius of the conductors
B. The distance between the centers of the conductors and the length of the line
C. The radius of the conductors and the frequency of the signal
D. The frequency of the signal and the length of the line

A The characteristic impedance of a parallel-conductor feed line depends on the distance between the conductor centers and the radius of the conductors.

ARRL0123

Two - Wire Line

$$Z_0 = 276 \: LOG \: \frac{2S}{d} \: OHMS$$

Figure G9-1 — You can calculate the characteristic impedance of parallel conductor feed line from the diameter of the conductors and the spacing between them.

Conductors

Dielectric (Insulator)

ARRL0124

Figure G9-2 — This drawing shows the construction of common 300-ohm twin lead. This is one form of parallel-conductor feed line.

G9A02   What is the typical characteristic impedance of coaxial cables used for antenna feedlines at amateur stations?

A. 25 and 30 ohms
B. 50 and 75 ohms
C. 80 and 100 ohms
D. 500 and 750 ohms

B   Common coaxial cables used as antenna feed lines have characteristic impedances of 50 or 75 ohms.

Outer Conductor (Braid)
Single-Shielded
ARRL0125
Center Conductor
Dielectric
Outer Insulation (Vinyl Jacket)

Figure G9-3 — Coaxial cables consist of a conductor surrounded by insulation called the dielectric. The second conductor, called the shield, goes around the dielectric. Plastic insulation goes around the entire cable.

G9A03   What is the characteristic impedance of flat ribbon TV type twin lead?

A. 50 ohms
B. 75 ohms
C. 100 ohms
D. 300 ohms

D   The flat ribbon type of feed line often used with TV antennas has a characteristic impedance of 300 ohms. This feed line is called twin lead. (See Figures G9-1 and G9-2 with question G9A01.)

G9A04 **What is a common reason for the occurrence of reflected power at the point where a feedline connects to an antenna?**

A. Operating an antenna at its resonant frequency
B. Using more transmitter power than the antenna can handle
C. A difference between feedline impedance and antenna feed point impedance
D. Feeding the antenna with unbalanced feedline

C Whenever power traveling along a feed line encounters a different impedance from the characteristic impedance of the feed line, such as at an antenna, some of the power is reflected back toward the power source. The greater the difference between the feed line's characteristic impedance and the new impedance, the larger the fraction of power that is reflected.

Power reflected back from an antenna returns to the transmitter, which in turn reflects the power back toward the antenna, creating a standing wave. When the transmitter and antenna impedances are not matched, less power is transferred to the antenna because of the extra loss incurred as the reflected power travels up and down the feed line.

G9A05 **What must be done to prevent standing waves on an antenna feedline?**

A. The antenna feed point must be at DC ground potential
B. The feedline must be cut to an odd number of electrical quarter wavelengths long
C. The feedline must be cut to an even number of physical half wavelengths long
D. The antenna feed point impedance must be matched to the characteristic impedance of the feedline

D To eliminate reflected power, the antenna impedance must be matched to the characteristic impedance of the feed line. If the impedances are matched, all of the feed line power is transferred to the antenna. The problem with reflected power causing standing waves and raising the feed line SWR is not generally transmitter efficiency, but rather the transmitter's reaction to the high SWR. Modern solid-state transmitters usually have protection circuitry that reduces the power output in the presence of high SWR. (When the SWR is high there are high voltages present that can damage components.) By reducing SWR, the transmitter can operate at maximum power output.

G9A06 Which of the following is a reason for using an inductively coupled matching network between the transmitter and parallel conductor feed line feeding an antenna?

A. To increase the radiation resistance
B. To reduce spurious emissions
C. To match the unbalanced transmitter output to the balanced parallel conductor feedline
D. To reduce the feed-point impedance of the antenna

C Most transmitters are designed to accommodate unbalanced coaxial cable. In order to use a balanced parallel-conductor feed line, a matching network should be used. An inductively coupled matching network can be a good choice for this application because it will also match the unbalanced transmitter output to the balanced feed line.

Figure G9-4 — An inductively coupled matching network for balanced feed lines.

G9A07 How does the attenuation of coaxial cable change as the frequency of the signal it is carrying increases?

A. It is independent of frequency
B. It increases
C. It decreases
D. It reaches a maximum at approximately 18 MHz

B Line loss is greater at higher frequencies. If you were to use the same type of coaxial cable feed line for your 160 meter antenna as for your 2 meter antenna, there would be much more loss at the 2 meter frequencies.

G9A08 In what values are RF feed line losses usually expressed?

A. ohms per 1000 ft
B. dB per 1000 ft
C. ohms per 100 ft
D. dB per 100 ft

D RF feed line loss is normally specified in decibels (dB) of loss for each 100 feet of line. Loss must also be specified at a certain frequency.

G9A09 What standing-wave-ratio will result from the connection of a 50-ohm feed line to a non-reactive load having a 200-ohm impedance?

A. 4:1
B. 1:4
C. 2:1
D. 1:2

A If a load on a feed line is purely resistive, the SWR can be calculated by dividing the line characteristic impedance by the load resistance or vice versa, whichever gives a value greater than one.

$$\frac{200}{50} = 4:1 \text{ SWR}$$

G9A10 What standing-wave-ratio will result from the connection of a 50-ohm feed line to a non-reactive load having a 10-ohm impedance?

A. 2:1
B. 50:1
C. 1:5
D. 5:1

D If a load on a feed line is purely resistive, the SWR can be calculated by dividing the line characteristic impedance by the load resistance or vice versa, whichever gives a value greater than one.

$$\frac{50}{10} = 5:1 \text{ SWR}$$

G9A11 What standing-wave-ratio will result from the connection of a 50-ohm feed line to a non-reactive load having a 50-ohm impedance?

A. 2:1
B. 1:1
C. 50:50
D. 0:0

B If a load on a feed line is purely resistive, the SWR can be calculated by dividing the line characteristic impedance by the load resistance or vice versa, whichever gives a value greater than one.

$$\frac{50}{50} = 1:1 \text{ SWR}$$

G9A12 **What would be the SWR if you feed a vertical antenna that has a 25-ohm feed-point impedance with 50-ohm coaxial cable?**

    A. 2:1

    B. 2.5:1

    C. 1.25:1

    D. You cannot determine SWR from impedance values

A   If a load on a feed line is purely resistive, the SWR can be calculated by dividing the line characteristic impedance by the load resistance or vice versa, whichever gives a value greater than one.

$$\frac{50}{25} = 2:1 \text{ SWR}$$

G9A13 **What would be the SWR if you feed a folded dipole antenna that has a 300-ohm feed-point impedance with 50-ohm coaxial cable?**

    A. 1.5:1

    B. 3:1

    C. 6:1

    D. You cannot determine SWR from impedance values

C   If a load on a feed line is purely resistive, the SWR can be calculated by dividing the line characteristic impedance by the load resistance or vice versa, whichever gives a value greater than one.

$$\frac{300}{50} = 6:1 \text{ SWR}$$

G9A14 **If the SWR on an antenna feedline is 5 to 1, and a matching network at the transmitter end of the feedline is adjusted to 1 to 1 SWR, what is the resulting SWR on the feedline?**

    A. 1 to 1

    B. 5 to 1

    C. Between 1 to 1 and 5 to 1 depending on the characteristic impedance of the line

    D. Between 1 to 1 and 5 to 1 depending on the reflected power at the transmitter

B   A matching network at the transmitter does not change the SWR on the feed line, so the feed line SWR is still 5:1.

G9B Basic antennas

G9B01 What is one disadvantage of a directly fed random-wire antenna?
A. It must be longer than 1 wavelength
B. You may experience RF burns when touching metal objects in your station
C. It produces vertically polarized radiation
D. It is not effective on the higher HF bands

B   A random-length wire antenna is often referred to as a random-wire antenna. It consists simply of a wire. A random-wire antenna can be of any length because an antenna tuner is used to match the impedances. It does not require a feed line because the single piece of wire serves as both a feed line and an antenna. It is considered to be a multiband antenna, because the antenna tuner will match the impedances for several frequency bands. One significant disadvantage of a random-wire antenna is that you may experience RF feedback in your station when using a random-length wire antenna because of the proximity of the radiating antenna to your equipment.

G9B02 What is an advantage of downward sloping radials on a ground-plane antenna?
A. They lower the radiation angle
B. They bring the feed-point impedance closer to 300 ohms
C. They increase the radiation angle
D. They can be adjusted to bring the feed-point impedance closer to 50 ohms

D   A ground-plane antenna has a ¼-wavelength vertical radiating element and four ¼-wavelength horizontal "radial" elements. You can change the impedance of a ground-plane antenna by changing the angle of the radials. Bending or sloping the radials downward to about a 45-degree angle will increase the impedance from approximately 35 ohms to approximately 50 ohms, resulting in lower SWR in the feed line.

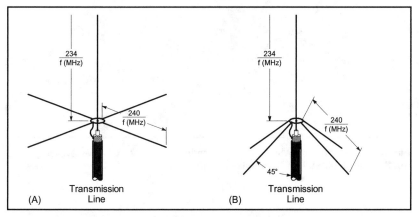

Figure G9-5 — A ground-plane antenna may use horizontal or downward-sloping radials.

G9B03   What happens to the feed-point impedance of a ground-plane antenna when its radials are changed from horizontal to downward-sloping?

A. It decreases
B. It increases
C. It stays the same
D. It reaches a maximum at an angle of 45 degrees

B   See the discussion for question G9B02

G9B04   What is the low angle azimuthal radiation pattern of an ideal half-wavelength dipole antenna installed ½ wavelength high and parallel to the earth?

A. It is a figure-eight at right angles to the antenna
B. It is a figure-eight off both ends of the antenna
C. It is a circle (equal radiation in all directions)
D. It has a pair of lobes on one side of the antenna and a single lobe on the other side

A   A ½-wavelength dipole antenna radiates its signals in a bidirectional fashion at a 90° angle to the antenna wires. This is called a "figure 8" radiation pattern. If the antenna is placed less than ½ wavelength above the ground, the ideal signal pattern will become distorted as more of the antenna's signal will be radiated at high vertical angles.

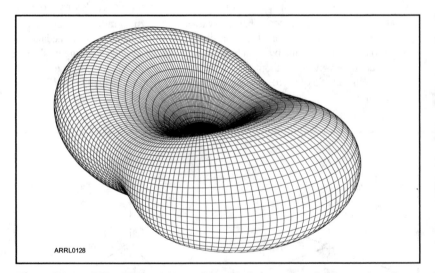

ARRL0128

Figure G9-6 — This drawing shows the radiation pattern of a ½-wavelength dipole antenna installed ½ wavelength above ground.

G9B05   How does antenna height affect the horizontal (azimuthal) radiation pattern of a horizontal dipole HF antenna?

A. If the antenna is too high, the pattern becomes unpredictable
B. Antenna height has no effect on the pattern
C. If the antenna is less than ½ wavelength high, the azimuthal pattern is almost omnidirectional
D. If the antenna is less than ½ wavelength high, radiation off the ends of the wire is eliminated

C   A ½-wavelength dipole antenna in free space radiates its signals in a bidirectional fashion at a 90° angle to the antenna wires. This is called a "figure 8" radiation pattern. If the antenna is placed less than ½ wavelength above the ground, the ideal signal pattern will become distorted. For heights of less than ½ wavelength, the antenna pattern becomes almost omnidirectional, sending signals nearly equally in all compass directions.

G9B06   Where should the radial wires of a ground-mounted vertical antenna system be placed?

A. As high as possible above the ground
B. Parallel to the antenna element
C. On the surface or buried a few inches below the ground
D. At the top of the antenna

C   In most installations, ground conductivity is inadequate, so an artificial ground must be made from wires placed along the ground near the base of the antenna. These wires, called radials, are usually ¼-wavelength or longer. Depending on ground conductivity, up to 30 or more radials may be required to form an effective ground. The radial wires of a ground-mounted vertical antenna should be placed on the ground surface or buried a few inches below the surface.

G9B07   How does the feed-point impedance of a ½ wave dipole antenna change as the antenna is lowered from ¼ wave above ground?

A. It steadily increases
B. It steadily decreases
C. It peaks at about ⅛ wavelength above ground
D. It is unaffected by the height above ground

B   As the antenna is lowered from ¼-wavelength above ground, the impedance steadily decreases to a very low value when placed directly on the ground.

G9B08 How does the feed-point impedance of a ½ wave dipole change as the feed-point location is moved from the center toward the ends?

A. It steadily increases
B. It steadily decreases
C. It peaks at about ⅛ wavelength from the end
D. It is unaffected by the location of the feed-point

A The center of a ½-wavelength dipole is the location of the lowest feed-point impedance, approximately 72 ohms in free space. At the ends of the dipole, feed-point impedance is several thousand ohms. In between, feed-point impedance increases steadily as the feed point is moved from the center toward the ends of the antenna.

G9B09 Which of the following is an advantage of a horizontally polarized as compared to vertically polarized HF antenna?

A. Lower ground reflection losses
B. Lower feed-point impedance
C. Shorter Radials
D. Lower radiation resistance

A Radio waves reflecting from the ground have lower losses when the polarization of the wave is parallel to the ground. That is, when the waves are horizontally polarized. Because the reflected waves combine with the direct waves (not reflected) to make up the antenna's radiation pattern, lower reflection loss results in stronger signal strength. Ground-mounted vertical antennas, however, are able to generate stronger signals at low angles of radiation than horizontally polarized antennas at low heights. This means they are often preferred for DX contacts on the lower HF bands where it is impractical to raise horizontally polarized antennas to the height necessary for strong low-angle signals.

G9B10 What is the approximate length for a ½-wave dipole antenna cut for 14.250 MHz?

A. 8.2 feet
B. 16.4 feet
C. 24.6 feet
D. 32.8 feet

D To calculate the length of a ½ wavelength dipole divide 468 by the frequency in MHz:

$$\text{Length (feet)} = \frac{468}{14.250} = 32.8 \text{ feet}$$

G9B11 **What is the approximate length for a ½-wave dipole antenna cut for 3.550 MHz?**

    A. 42.2 feet

    B. 84.5 feet

    C. 131.8 feet

    D. 263.6 feet

C   To calculate the length of a ½ wavelength dipole divide 468 by the frequency in MHz:

$$\text{Length (feet)} = \frac{468}{3.550} = 131.8 \text{ feet}$$

G9B12 **What is the approximate length for a ¼-wave vertical antenna cut for 28.5 MHz?**

    A. 8.2 feet

    B. 10.5 feet

    C. 16.4 feet

    D. 21.0 feet

A   To calculate the length of a ¼ wavelength vertical divide 234 by the frequency in MHz:

$$\text{Length (feet)} = \frac{234}{28.5} = 8.2 \text{ feet}$$

G9C   Directional antennas

G9C01   How can the SWR bandwidth of a Yagi antenna be increased?
- A. Use larger diameter elements
- B. Use closer element spacing
- C. Use traps on the elements
- D. Use tapered-diameter elements

A   Using larger diameter elements can increase the SWR bandwidth of a parasitic beam antenna, such as a Yagi antenna. The exact length of the elements becomes less critical when larger diameter elements are used.

G9C02   What is the approximate length of the driven element of a Yagi antenna?
- A. ¼ wavelength
- B. ½ wavelength
- C. ¾ wavelength
- D. 1 wavelength

B   The driven element of the Yagi antenna is very similar to a ½-wavelength dipole.

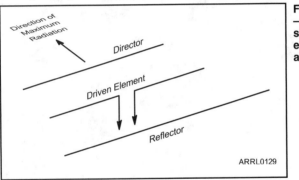

Figure G9-7 — This drawing shows a three-element Yagi antenna.

G9C03   Which statement about a three-element single-band Yagi antenna is true?
- A. The reflector is normally the shortest parasitic element
- B. The director is normally the shortest parasitic element
- C. The driven element is the longest parasitic element
- D. Low feed-point impedance increases bandwidth

B   In a typical Yagi, the director is 95% of the length of the driven element and is placed in front of the driven element in the direction signals are to be transmitted and received. The reflector element is 105% of the length of the driven element and is placed to the rear. The director is normally the shortest element of a Yagi antenna. (See Figure G9-7 with question G9C02.)

G9C04 Which statement about a Yagi antenna is true?

A. The reflector is normally the longest parasitic element
B. The director is normally the longest parasitic element
C. The reflector is normally the shortest parasitic element
D. All of the elements must be the same length

A See the discussion for question G9C03.

G9C05 What is one effect of increasing the boom length and adding directors to a Yagi antenna?

A. Gain increases
B. SWR increases
C. Weight decreases
D. Wind load decreases

A As the boom length of a Yagi is increased and more elements are added, the directivity or gain of the antenna increases. Directivity has an advantage in that it concentrates the transmitted and received signals in the intended direction more than in other directions, thus minimizing interference.

G9C06 Which of the following is a reason why a Yagi antenna is often used for radio communications on the 20 meter band?

A. It provides excellent omnidirectional coverage in the horizontal plane
B. It is smaller, less expensive and easier to erect than a dipole or vertical antenna
C. It helps reduce interference from other stations to the side or behind the antenna
D. It provides the highest possible angle of radiation for the HF bands

C A Yagi antenna provides gain or directivity. Directivity has an advantage in that it concentrates the transmitted and received signals in the intended direction more than in other directions. Directivity applies to receiving as well as transmitting, so the antenna picks up signals better from the desired direction and rejects signals coming from the sides or back of the antenna. This minimizes interference from stations in other directions. This is one important reason for using a Yagi antenna for HF operation, such as on the 20-meter band.

G9C07 What does "front-to-back ratio" mean in reference to a Yagi antenna?

A. The number of directors versus the number of reflectors
B. The relative position of the driven element with respect to the reflectors and directors
C. The power radiated in the major radiation lobe compared to the power radiated in exactly the opposite direction
D. The ratio of forward gain to dipole gain

C Using a directional antenna helps reduce interference in that it sends the signal in the intended direction, rather than off to the side or behind. Most of the radiated signal is sent in the desired direction. This is called the major lobe, or main lobe, of the antenna's radiation pattern. A much smaller amount of the signal is radiated in other directions. If you measure the power radiated in the major lobe (or in the desired direction) and compare that with the power radiated in the exact opposite direction, you have a measure of the antenna "front-to-back ratio."

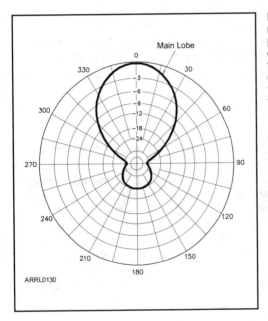

Figure G9-8 — This diagram represents the directive pattern for a typical three-element Yagi antenna. Note that this pattern is essentially unidirectional, with most of the radiation in the direction of the main lobe. There is also a small *minor lobe* at 180° from the direction of the main lobe, however. You can read the front-to-back-ratio on this type of graph by finding the strength of the minor lobe off the back of the antenna. For this antenna, the front-to-back-ratio is 24 dB because the maximum signal at 180° just touches the −24 dB circle. That means the signal off the back of the antenna is 24 dB less than the signal from the front or forward direction of the antenna.

G9C08   What is meant by the "main lobe" of a directive antenna?

A. The magnitude of the maximum vertical angle of radiation
B. The point of maximum current in a radiating antenna element
C. The maximum voltage standing wave point on a radiating element
D. The direction of maximum radiated field strength from the antenna

D   A Yagi antenna radiates most of the signal in the desired direction. This is called the major lobe, or main lobe, of the antenna's radiation pattern. A much smaller amount of the signal is radiated in other directions. (See Figure G9-8 and the discussion for question G9C07.)

G9C09   What is the approximate maximum theoretical gain of a 3 element Yagi antenna?

A. 9.7 dBi
B. 7.3 dBd
C. 5.4 times the gain of a dipole
D. All of these choices are correct

A   The maximum theoretical gain of a 3-element Yagi antenna is 9.7 dBi. The term "dBi" means "decibels with respect to an isotropic antenna." An isotropic antenna is one that radiates equally in all possible directions.

G9C10   Which of the following is a Yagi antenna design variable that could be adjusted to optimize forward gain, front-to-back ratio, or SWR bandwidth?

A. The physical length of the boom
B. The number of elements on the boom
C. The spacing of each element along the boom
D. All of these choices are correct

D   All of these choices affect a Yagi antenna's forward gain, front-to-back ratio, and SWR bandwidth. As you might imagine, adjusting an antenna design for the desired combination of these three important parameters can be a complicated procedure. Computer modeling programs greatly simplify this process.

G9C11   What is the purpose of a "gamma match" used with Yagi antennas?

A. To match the relatively low feed-point impedance to 50 ohms
B. To match the relatively high feed-point impedance to 50 ohms
C. To increase the front to back ratio
D. To increase the main lobe gain

A   A gamma match transforms the relatively low feed-point impedance of a Yagi's driven element (typically 25 ohms or less) to 50 ohms to match the characteristic impedance of common coaxial feed lines.

G9C12 Which of the following describes a common method for insulating the driven element of a Yagi antenna from the metal boom when using a gamma match?

A. Support the driven element with ceramic standoff insulators
B. Insert a high impedance transformer at the driven element
C. Insert a high voltage balun at the driven element
D. None of these answers are correct. No insulation in needed

D One major advantage of the gamma match is that the driven element does not have to be insulated from the antenna's boom. This simplifies mounting the element and leads to a sturdier antenna.

G9C13 Approximately how long is each side of a cubical-quad antenna driven element?

A. ¼ wavelength
B. ½ wavelength
C. ¾ wavelength
D. 1 wavelength

A All of the elements of a cubical-quad antenna are square-shaped loops. The entire driven element of a cubical-quad antenna is approximately a full wavelength, so each of the 4 sides is approximately ¼ wavelength.

No. 12 wire

$$\text{Reflector (overall ft)} = \frac{1030}{f\,(\text{MHz})}$$

Reflector

0.15λ to 0.2λ

Driven Element

Bamboo or Fiberglass Spreaders

Short

Tuning Stub

Insulator

$$\text{Driven element (overall ft)} = \frac{1005}{f\,(\text{MHz})}$$

1/4 λ 75 Ω Coax

50 Ω Coax to Transmitter

ARRL0131

Figure G9-9 — This drawing shows the construction of a cubical-quad antenna. The lengths of the driven element and reflector element are given by the equations shown in the drawing. To find the length of one side, divide these total lengths by 4.

G9C14 How does the forward gain of a 2-element cubical-quad antenna compare to the forward gain of a 3 element Yagi antenna?

A. 2/3
B. About the same
C. 3/2
D. Twice

B A two-element quad (or delta loop) antenna has about the same gain as a three-element Yagi.

G9C15 Approximately how long is each side of a cubical-quad antenna reflector element?

A. Slightly less than ¼ wavelength
B. Slightly more than ¼ wavelength
C. Slightly less than ½ wavelength
D. Slightly more than ½ wavelength

B The reflector element of a cubical-quad antenna is slightly more than a full wavelength (about 1.025 times longer), so each of the 4 sides is slightly longer than ¼ wavelength. (See also Figure G9-9 and the discussion for question G9C13.)

G9C16 How does the gain of a two element delta-loop beam compare to the gain of a two element cubical quad antenna?

A. 3 dB higher
B. 3 dB lower
C. 2.54 dB higher
D. About the same

D Like the cubical quad antenna, a delta-loop antenna uses loop elements that are approximately one wavelength long. The difference is that delta loop elements are triangle-shaped loops, rather than square. The gain of a delta loop is about the same as a quad antenna when the number of elements and spacing are the same.

G9C17 **Approximately how long is each leg of a symmetrical delta-loop antenna Driven element?**

- A. ¼ wavelengths
- B. ⅓ wavelengths
- C. ½ wavelengths
- D. ⅔ wavelengths

B A delta-loop antenna has a driven element that is a triangle-shaped loop. It also uses a triangle-shaped loop reflector and sometimes one or more directors. The entire driven element of a delta-loop antenna is approximately a full wavelength, so each of the 3 sides is approximately ⅓ wavelength.

ARRL0132

Figure G9-10 — This drawing shows the construction of a delta-loop antenna. The lengths of the driven element and reflector element are given by the equations shown in the drawing. To find the length of one side, divide these total lengths by 3.

G9C18 Which of the following antenna types consists of a driven element and some combination of parasitically excited reflector and/or director elements?

A. A collinear array
B. A rhombic antenna
C. A double-extended Zepp antenna
D. A Yagi antenna

D The driven element of a Yagi antenna is connected to the feed line. The remaining elements are parasitic in that they operate by collecting and re-radiating some of the energy radiated by the driven element without a direct connection to the feed line. Elements that reinforce the radiated signal in the desired direction are called directors. Elements that reflect the signal toward the desired direction are called reflectors.

G9C19 What type of directional antenna is typically constructed from 2 square loops of wire each having a circumference of approximately one wavelength at the operating frequency and separated by approximately 0.2 wavelength?

A. A stacked dipole array
B. A collinear array
C. A cubical quad antenna
D. An Adcock array

C See the discussion for question G9C13 and Figure G9-9.

G9C20 What happens when the feed-point of a cubical quad antenna is changed from the center of the lowest horizontal wire to the center of one of the vertical wires?

A. The polarization of the radiated signal changes from horizontal to vertical
B. The polarization of the radiated signal changes from vertical to horizontal
C. The direction of the main lobe is reversed
D. The radiated signal changes to an omnidirectional pattern

A Polarization from a vertically-oriented 1-wavelength loop is determined by where the feed point is located. If the feed point is located at the top or bottom of the loop, the polarization of the radiated signal is horizontal. If the feed point is located on either side of the loop, the polarization of the radiated signal is vertical.

G9C21   What configuration of the loops of a cubical-quad antenna must be used for the antenna to operate as a beam antenna, assuming one of the elements is used as a reflector?

   A. The driven element must be fed with a balun transformer
   B. The driven element must be open-circuited on the side opposite the feed-point
   C. The reflector element must be approximately 5% shorter than the driven element
   D. The reflector element must be approximately 5% longer than the driven element

D   The reflector element of a cubical-quad antenna is slightly more than a full wavelength (about 1.025 times longer), so each of the 4 sides is slightly longer than $\frac{1}{4}$ wavelength. (See also the discussion for question G9C13 and Figure G9-9.)

G9D   Specialized antennas

G9D01   What does the term "NVIS" mean as related to antennas?

   A. Nearly Vertical Inductance System
   B. Non-Visible Installation Specification
   C. Non-Varying Impedance Smoothing
   D. Near Vertical Incidence Skywave

D   NVIS, or Near Vertical Incidence Skywave, refers to a communications system that uses low, horizontally polarized antennas such as dipoles that radiate most of their signal at high vertical angles. These signals are then reflected back to Earth in a region centered on the antenna. NVIS allows stations to communicate within the skip zone for lower-angle sky wave propagation.

G9D02   Which of the following is an advantage of an NVIS antenna?

   A. Low vertical angle radiation for DX work
   B. High vertical angle radiation for short skip during the day
   C. High forward gain
   D. All of these choices are correct

B   See the discussion for question G9D01.

G9D03   At what height above ground is an NVIS antenna typically installed?

   A. As close to one-half wave as possible
   B. As close to one wavelength as possible
   C. Height is not critical as long as significantly more than $\frac{1}{2}$ wavelength
   D. Between $\frac{1}{10}$ and $\frac{1}{4}$ wavelength

D   NVIS must be mounted close to the ground so that the radiated signal is maximized at high vertical angles.

G9D04 How does the gain of two 3-element horizontally polarized Yagi antennas spaced vertically ½ wave apart from each other typically compare to the gain of a single 3-element Yagi?

A. Approximately 1.5 dB higher
B. Approximately 3 dB higher
C. Approximately 6 dB higher
D. Approximately 9 dB higher

B "Stacking" two Yagis the proper distance apart combines their signals so that the forward gain of the resulting array is doubled, a gain of 3 dB.

G9D05 What is the advantage of vertical stacking of horizontally polarized Yagi antennas?

A. Allows quick selection of vertical or horizontal polarization
B. Allows simultaneous vertical and horizontal polarization
C. Narrows the main lobe in azimuth
D. Narrows the main lobe in elevation

D The increase in gain for a vertical stack of Yagi antennas results from narrowing the main or major lobe of a single antenna's radiation pattern. The narrower lobe results in stronger received signals and less received noise at angles away from the peak of the main lobe. (See also the discussion for G9D04.)

G9D06 Which of the following is an advantage of a log periodic antenna?

A. Wide bandwidth
B. Higher gain per element than a Yagi antenna
C. Harmonic suppression
D. Polarization diversity

A A log periodic antenna is designed to provide consistent gain and feed-point impedance over a wide frequency range.

G9D07 Which of the following describes a log periodic antenna?

A. Length and spacing of elements increases logarithmically from one end of the boom to the other
B. Impedance varies periodically as a function of frequency
C. Gain varies logarithmically as a function of frequency
D. SWR varies periodically as a function of boom length

A The name "log-periodic" refers to the ratio of length and spacing between adjacent elements of the antenna. By designing the antenna entirely in terms of ratios, the antenna's performance becomes independent of frequency over a wide range.

G9D08　Why is a Beverage antenna generally not used for transmitting?

A. Its impedance is too low for effective matching
B. It has high losses compared to other types of antennas
C. It has poor directivity
D. All of these choices are correct

B　The Beverage antenna is used for receiving because it rejects noise and signals from unwanted directions, increasing the received signal-to-noise ratio for better copying ability. It is not used for transmitting because it is quite lossy compared to most transmitting antennas.

G9D09　Which of the following is an application for a Beverage antenna?

A. Directional transmitting for low HF bands
B. Directional receiving for low HF bands
C. Portable Direction finding at higher HF frequencies
D. Portable Direction finding at lower HF frequencies

B　Beverage antennas are most effective at frequencies of 7 MHz and below. This includes the amateur MF 160 meter band, as well as the lower HF bands of 80, 60 and 40 meters.

G9D10　Which of the following describes a Beverage antenna?

A. A vertical antenna constructed from beverage cans
B. A broad-band mobile antenna
C. A helical antenna for space reception
D. A very long and low receiving antenna that is highly directional

D　The typical Beverage antenna consists of a wire 1-wavelength or more long, supported from 6 to 10 feet above ground. It is terminated with a 300-1000 ohm resistor connected to a ground rod at the end of the antenna in the direction of preferred reception. It is highly directional, rejecting noise and signals from unwanted directions.

G9D11 **Which of the following is a disadvantage of multiband antennas?**

A. They present low impedance on all design frequencies
B. They must be used with an antenna tuner
C. They must be fed with open wire line
D. They have poor harmonic rejection

D Multiband antennas by definition are designed to radiate well on several frequencies. Most HF amateur bands are harmonically-related, meaning their frequencies are integral multiples of each other — 3.5, 7, 14, 21 and 28 MHz. While this is convenient in that one antenna can be used on separate bands, harmonics of a fundamental signal on, for example 7 MHz, will be radiated well by a multiband antenna on 14, 21 and 28 MHz.

G9D12 **What is the primary purpose of traps installed in antennas?**

A. To permit multiband operation
B. To notch spurious frequencies
C. To provide balanced feed-point impedance
D. To prevent out of band operation

A Traps, consisting of parallel LC circuits, act as electrical switches to isolate sections of the antenna at their resonant frequencies. At other frequencies, traps act as inductance or capacitance. This changes the antenna's "electrical length" automatically, allowing it to operate on two or more bands.

Electrical and RF Safety

Your General class exam (Element 3) will consist of 35 questions taken from the General class question pool as prepared by the Volunteer Examiner Coordinators' Question Pool Committee. A certain number of questions are taken from each of the 10 subelements. There will be 2 questions from the subelement shown in this chapter. These questions are divided into 2 groups, labeled G0A and G0B.

G0A   RF safety principles, rules, and guidelines; routine station evaluation

G0A01   What is one way that RF energy can affect human body tissue?
A. It heats body tissue
B. It causes radiation poisoning
C. It causes the blood count to reach a dangerously low level
D. It cools body tissue

A   Body tissues that are subjected to very high levels of RF energy may suffer heat damage. These effects depend on the frequency of the energy, the power density of the RF field that strikes the body, and even on factors such as the polarization of the wave. The thermal effects of RF energy should not be a major concern for most radio amateurs because of the relatively low RF power we normally use and the intermittent nature of most amateur transmissions. It is rare for amateurs to be subjected to RF fields strong enough to produce thermal effects unless they are fairly close to an energized antenna or unshielded power amplifier.

G0A02   Which property is NOT important in estimating if an RF signal exceeds the maximum permissible exposure (MPE)?
A. Its duty cycle
B. Its critical angle
C. Its power density
D. Its frequency

B   The body's natural resonant frequencies affect how the body absorbs RF energy. For this reason, polarization, power density and the frequency of the radio signal are all important in estimating the effects of RF energy on body tissue. The critical angle refers to an entirely different, unrelated concept. It is the maximum angle above the horizon at which a radio signal will be returned to the earth.

G0A03 **Which of the following has the most direct effect on the permitted exposure level of RF radiation?**

A. The age of the person exposed
B. The power level and frequency of the energy
C. The environment near the transmitter
D. The type of transmission line used

B   The heating effect of RF on the body depends upon the frequency (or wavelength) of the energy, the power density of the RF field that strikes the body, and even on factors such as polarization of the wave. Of those factors, the power level and frequency of the RF energy are the most significant.

G0A04 **What does "time averaging" mean in reference to RF radiation exposure?**

A. The average time of day when the exposure occurs
B. The average time it takes RF radiation to have any long-term effect on the body
C. The total time of the exposure
D. The total RF exposure averaged over a certain time

D   Time averaging, when applied to RF radiation exposure, takes into account the total RF exposure averaged over either a 6-minute or a 30-minute exposure time. Time averaging compensates for the transmit/receive time ratio during normal amateur communications. It takes into account that the body cools itself after a time of reduced or no radiation exposure.

G0A05 **What must you do if an evaluation of your station shows RF energy radiated from your station exceeds permissible limits?**

A. Take action to prevent human exposure to the excessive RF fields
B. File an Environmental Impact Statement (EIS-97) with the FCC
C. Secure written permission from your neighbors to operate above the controlled MPE limits
D. All of these answers are correct

A   Some of the things you can do to prevent human exposure to excessive RF radiation are to move your antennas farther away, restrict access to the areas where exposure would exceed the limits, or reduce transmitter power to reduce the field strengths in those areas.

GOA06 **Which transmitter(s) at a multiple user site is/are responsible for RF safety compliance?**

A. Only the most powerful transmitter on site
B. All transmitters on site, regardless of their power level or duty cycle
C. Any transmitter that contributes 5% or more of the MPE
D. Only those that operate at more than 50% duty cycle

C In a multi-transmitter environment, each transmitter operator may be jointly responsible (with all other site operators) for ensuring that the total RF exposure from the site does not exceed the MPE limits. Any transmitter (including the antenna) that produces more than 5% of the total permissible exposure limit for transmissions at that frequency must be included in the site evaluation. (This is 5% of the permitted power density or 5% of the square of the E or H-field MPE limit. It is *not* 5% of the total exposure, which sometimes can be unknown.) The situation described by this question is common for amateur repeater installations, which often share a transmitting site with other transmitters in commercial radio services.

GOA07 **What effect does transmitter duty cycle have when evaluating RF exposure?**

A. A lower transmitter duty cycle permits greater short-term exposure levels
B. A higher transmitter duty cycle permits greater short-term exposure levels
C. Low duty cycle transmitters are exempt from RF exposure evaluation requirements
D. Only those transmitters that operate at a 100% duty cycle must be evaluated

A Since amateurs usually spend more time listening than transmitting, low duty cycles are common. Remember that including duty cycle in the exposure evaluation takes into account the reduced average transmitted power from not operating continuously at full power. This means greater short-term exposure levels can be permitted with low-duty-cycle emissions.

GOA08 **Which of the following steps must an amateur operator take to ensure compliance with RF safety regulations?**

A. Post a copy of FCC Part 97 in the station
B. Post a copy of OET Bulletin 65 in the station
C. Perform a routine RF exposure evaluation
D. All of these choices are correct

C Even if your station is exempt from the requirement, you may want to do a simple RF Radiation Exposure Evaluation. The results would demonstrate to you and possibly to your neighbors that your station is within the guidelines and is no cause for concern. None of the actions listed in the other answer choices would help to ensure that your station meets the FCC RF safety regulations.

G0A09 **What type of instrument can be used to accurately measure an RF field?**

A. A receiver with an S meter
B. A calibrated field-strength meter with a calibrated antenna
C. A betascope with a dummy antenna calibrated at 50 ohms
D. An oscilloscope with a high-stability crystal marker generator

B You can use a calibrated field-strength meter and calibrated field-strength sensor (antenna) to accurately measure an RF field. Even if you have access to such an expensive laboratory-grade field-strength meter, several factors can upset the readings. Reflections from the ground and nearby conductors (power lines, other antennas, house wiring and so on) can easily confuse field-strength readings. You must know the frequency response of the test equipment and probes, and use them only within the appropriate range. Even the orientation of the test probe with respect to the polarization of the antenna being tested is important.

G0A10 **What do the RF safety rules require when the maximum power output capability of an otherwise compliant station is reduced?**

A. Filing of the changes with the FCC
B. Recording of the power level changes in the log or station records
C. Performance of a routine RF exposure evaluation
D. No further action is required

D Any time you make changes to your station you should decide if you have done anything to increase the RF exposure to any area. Regardless of whether you need to do a new evaluation or not, your station must always comply with the RF safety rules. In the example given in this question, you would not need to perform an RF safety evaluation because you know your station was in compliance with the MPE limits at the higher power, so you can be fairly certain that it will still comply at the lower power. If you also made other significant changes, such as going from a dipole antenna to a high-gain beam antenna, then you may need to perform an evaluation.

G0A11 **What precaution should you take if you install an indoor transmitting antenna?**

A. Locate the antenna close to your operating position to minimize feed line radiation
B. Position the antenna along the edge of a wall to reduce parasitic radiation
C. Make sure that MPE limits are not exceeded in occupied areas
D. No special precautions are necessary if SSB and CW are the only modes used

C You should locate any antenna (whether it is indoors or outdoors) as far away as practical from living spaces that will be occupied while you are operating. You should also perform a routine environmental evaluation to make sure that MPE limits are not exceeded in occupied areas.

G0A12 **What precaution should you take whenever you make adjustments or repairs to an antenna?**

A. Ensure that you and the antenna structure are grounded
B. Turn off the transmitter and disconnect the feedline
C. Wear a radiation badge
D. All of these answers are correct

B One way to be sure that no one can activate the transmitter while you are working on it is to turn off the transmitter power supply and disconnect the antenna feed line. If there is a chance of anyone entering the station, it is also a good idea to post a notice that you are working on the antenna.

G0A13 **What precaution should be taken when installing a ground-mounted antenna?**

A. It should not be installed higher than you can reach
B. It should not be installed in a wet area
C. It should be painted so people or animals do not accidentally run into it
D. It should be installed so no one can be exposed to RF radiation in excess of maximum permissible limits

D No one should be near a transmitting antenna while it is in use. Install ground-mounted transmitting antennas well away from living areas so that people cannot come close enough to be exposed to more than the MPE limits. If there is a possibility of someone walking up to your antenna while you are transmitting, it may be a good idea to install a protective fence around the antenna.

G0A14 **What is one thing that can be done if evaluation shows that a neighbor might receive more than the allowable limit of RF exposure from the main lobe of a directional antenna?**

A. Change from horizontal polarization to vertical polarization
B. Change from horizontal polarization to circular polarization
C. Use an antenna with a higher front-to-back ratio
D. Take precautions to ensure that the antenna cannot be pointed at their house

D A simple way to ensure that you do not point your antenna toward a neighbor's house while you are transmitting is to clearly mark your rotator control to remind you. Some rotator controls also have programmable "no go" regions that can prevent rotating the antenna to those directions.

G0A15 How can you determine that your station complies with FCC RF exposure regulations?

A. By calculation based on FCC OET Bulletin 65
B. By calculation based on computer modeling
C. By measurement of field strength using calibrated equipment
D. All of these choices are correct

D You may use any of these three procedures to determine whether your station complies with the exposure guidelines. The simplest, by far, is to perform the calculations in FCC OET Bulletin 65. There are on-line and software tools to help you perform the calculations. In complex or unique situations, it may be necessary to model or measure the exposure. [97.13(c)(1)]

G0B Safety in the ham shack: electrical shock and treatment, grounding, fusing, interlocks, wiring, antenna and tower safety

G0B01 Which wire(s) in a four-conductor line cord should be attached to fuses or circuit breakers in a device operated from a 240-VAC single-phase source?

A. Only the "hot" (black and red) wires
B. Only the "neutral" (white) wire
C. Only the ground (bare) wire
D. All wires

A The hot wires are the only ones that should be fused. If fuses are installed in the neutral or ground lines, an overload will open the fuses or circuit breaker but will *not* remove voltage from any equipment connected to that circuit.

G0B02 What is the minimum wire size that may be safely used for a circuit that draws up to 20 amperes of continuous current?

A. AWG number 20
B. AWG number 16
C. AWG number 12
D. AWG number 8

C Number 12 wire is required for a 20 ampere circuit.

G0B03 Which size of fuse or circuit breaker would be appropriate to use with a circuit that uses AWG number 14 wiring?

A. 100 amperes
B. 60 amperes
C. 30 amperes
D. 15 amperes

D Number 14 wiring should be protected by a 15 ampere fuse or circuit breaker.

G0B04 What is the mechanism by which electrical shock can be lethal?

A. Current through the heart can cause the heart to stop pumping
B. A large voltage field can induce currents in the brain
C. Heating effects in major organs can cause organ failure
D. All of these choices are correct

A The most lethal effect of current through the body is to disrupt the heart's natural pumping rhythm. Currents of more than 100 mA can cause the heart to completely stop or to enter an uncoordinated state called fibrillation. In either case, the loss of blood pressure leads to immediate unconsciousness and if the heart is not restarted, death.

G0B05 Which of the following conditions will cause a Ground Fault Circuit Interrupter (GFCI) to disconnect the 120 or 240 Volt AC line power to a device?

A. Current flowing from the hot wire to the neutral wire
B. Current flowing from the hot wire to ground
C. Over-voltage on the hot wire
D. All of these choices are correct

B A GFCI opens the circuit if it detects an imbalance in the currents flowing through the hot and neutral leads. The imbalance indicates that a leakage path exists from the hot connection to safety ground. That is a serious shock hazard, and it should be located and repaired.

G0B06 Why must the metal chassis of every item of station equipment be grounded (assuming the item has such a chassis)?

A. It prevents blowing of fuses in case of an internal short circuit
B. It provides a ground reference for the internal circuitry
C. It ensures that the neutral wire is grounded
D. It ensures that hazardous voltages cannot appear on the chassis

D Grounding the metal chassis provides a path for current if there is a short circuit between the hot or neutral leads and the equipment enclosure. Without a ground connection, a shock hazard may exist if the chassis is touched.

G0B07 Which of the following should be observed for safety when climbing on a tower using a safety belt or harness?

A. Never lean back and rely on the belt alone to support your weight
B. Always attach the belt safety hook to the belt "D" ring with the hook opening away from the tower
C. Ensure that all heavy tools are securely fastened to the belt D ring
D. Make sure that your belt is grounded at all times

B When climbing, make sure that hooks and clips are fully latched before putting any weight on them. Then be sure that for spring-loaded devices, the gate of the hook or clip can not be opened by pressing against the tower or hardware. You might not notice that it has been accidentally unlatched!

GOB08 What should be done by any person preparing to climb a tower that supports electrically powered devices?

A. Notify the electric company that a person will be working on the tower
B. Make sure all circuits that supply power to the tower are locked out and tagged
C. Ground the base of the tower
D. Disconnect the feed-line for every antenna at the station

B Before climbing, remove power from any circuit that will not be used while you are on the tower. The best way is to remove fuses or open circuit breakers. Once the circuit is opened, lock the circuit breaker open, if possible, and tag the fuse block or breaker panel so that no one will reconnect the circuit.

GOB09 Why is it not safe to use soldered joints with the wires that connect the base of a tower to a system of ground rods?

A. The resistance of solder is too high
B. Solder flux will prevent a low conductivity connection
C. Solder has too high a dielectric constant to provide adequate lightning protection
D. A soldered joint will be destroyed by the heat of a lightning strike

D When lightning strikes, the high current will melt the solder instantly and disconnect the ground wires. The proper way to bond ground wires to a tower is with a mechanical ground clamp.

GOB10 Which of the following is a danger from lead-tin solder?

A. Lead can contaminate food if hands are not washed carefully after handling
B. High voltages can cause lead-tin solder to disintegrate suddenly
C. Tin in the solder can "cold flow" causing shorts in the circuit
D. RF energy can convert the lead into a poisonous gas

A Lead is a known toxin when ingested or inhaled. Although the amount of soldering done by most amateurs does not cause enough lead exposure to be a hazard, it is a good idea to wash your hands after soldering and not eat "at the bench."

GOB11 Which of the following is good engineering practice for lightning protection grounds?

A. They must be bonded to all buried water and gas lines
B. Bends in ground wires must be made as close as possible to a right angle
C. Lightning grounds must be connected to all ungrounded wiring
D. They must be bonded together with all other grounds

D Lightning protection grounds must be tied to all other safety grounds in your home and shack. Having separate ground systems can expose equipment to damage from the lightning current surge jumping between ground systems.

G0B12 **What is the purpose of a transmitter power supply interlock?**

A. To prevent unauthorized access to a transmitter
B. To guarantee that you cannot accidentally transmit out of band
C. To ensure that dangerous voltages are removed if the cabinet is opened
D. To shut off the transmitter if too much current is drawn

C High voltages are often present inside transmitter and amplifier power supplies. The interlocks on those supplies prevent you from coming in contact with energized power supply components. Interlocks often short high voltage circuits to ground when activated, providing further safety measures. Do not defeat or bypass interlock circuits unless the repair instructions specifically require you to do so.

G0B13 **Which of the following is the most hazardous type of electrical energy?**

A. Direct Current
B. 60 cycle Alternating current
C. Radio Frequency
D. All of these choices are correct

B Low frequency alternating current at 50 or 60 Hz is the most hazardous because it penetrates the body easily and can disrupt the heart's natural pumping rhythm. (See also the discussion for question G0B04.)

G0B14 **What is the maximum amount of electrical current flow through the human body that can be tolerated safely?**

A. 5 microamperes
B. 50 microamperes
C. 500 milliamperes
D. 5 amperes

B The maximum level of current that has been shown to have no adverse affects is 50 microamperes.

Please Patronize ARRL Advertisers.
Support Those Who Support ARRL!

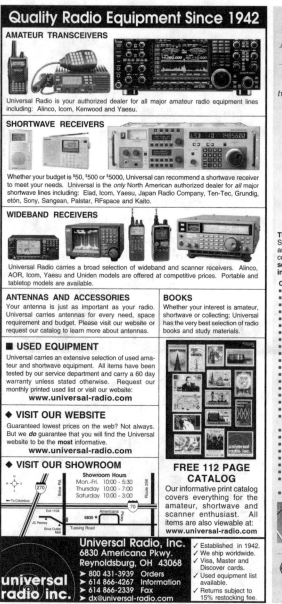

The ARRL General Q&A

KENWOOD
Listen to the Future

KENWOOD SKYCOMMAND
TURN IT ON!

Kenwood SkyCommand has FCC approval.

Allows Global communication through remote operation on HF frequencies at home or in the field utilizing Kenwood's TS-2000 series transceivers.

Kenwood's TH-D7AG or TM-D700A required for remote use.

Perfect for use in hurricane or tornado zones, as well as Search and Rescue areas for Long Distance Communications when other normal modes of communications are out.

A great tool to monitor propagation while doing other things at home!

No cables or adaptors to fool with or buy!

No software or computer required!!

Step by step setup and programming taking only minutes.

Ease of use.

See your local dealer for details.

KENWOOD U.S.A. CORPORATION
Communications Sector Headquarters
3975 Johns Creek Court, Suite 300, Suwanee, GA 30024-1265
Customer Support/Distribution
P.O. Box 22745, 2201 East Dominguez St., Long Beach, CA 90801-5745
Customer Support: (310) 639-4200   Fax: (310) 537-8235

INTERNET
Kenwood News & Products
http://www.kenwoodusa.com
ISO9001 Registered

About the ARRL _____

The seed for Amateur Radio was planted in the 1890s, when Guglielmo Marconi began his experiments in wireless telegraphy. Soon he was joined by dozens, then hundreds, of others who were enthusiastic about sending and receiving messages through the air—some with a commercial interest, but others solely out of a love for this new communications medium. The United States government began licensing Amateur Radio operators in 1912.

By 1914, there were thousands of Amateur Radio operators—hams—in the United States. Hiram Percy Maxim, a leading Hartford, Connecticut inventor and industrialist, saw the need for an organization to band together this fledgling group of radio experimenters. In May 1914 he founded the American Radio Relay League (ARRL) to meet that need.

Today ARRL, with approximately 150,000 members, is the largest organization of radio amateurs in the United States. The ARRL is a not-for-profit organization that:

- promotes interest in Amateur Radio communications and experimentation
- represents US radio amateurs in legislative matters, and
- maintains fraternalism and a high standard of conduct among Amateur Radio operators.

At ARRL headquarters in the Hartford suburb of Newington, the staff helps serve the needs of members. ARRL is also International Secretariat for the International Amateur Radio Union, which is made up of similar societies in 150 countries around the world.

ARRL publishes the monthly journal *QST*, as well as newsletters and many publications covering all aspects of Amateur Radio. Its headquarters station, W1AW, transmits bulletins of interest to radio amateurs and Morse code practice sessions. The ARRL also coordinates an extensive field organization, which includes volunteers who provide technical information and other support services for radio amateurs as well as communications for public-service activities. In addition, ARRL represents US amateurs with the Federal Communications Commission and other government agencies in the US and abroad.

Membership in ARRL means much more than receiving *QST* each month. In addition to the services already described, ARRL offers membership services on a personal level, such as the ARRL Volunteer Examiner Coordinator Program and a QSL bureau.

Full ARRL membership (available only to licensed radio amateurs) gives you a voice in how the affairs of the organization are governed.

ARRL policy is set by a Board of Directors (one from each of 15 Divisions). Each year, one-third of the ARRL Board of Directors stands for election by the full members they represent. The day-to-day operation of ARRL HQ is managed by an Executive Vice President and his staff.

No matter what aspect of Amateur Radio attracts you, ARRL membership is relevant and important. There would be no Amateur Radio as we know it today were it not for the ARRL. We would be happy to welcome you as a member! (An Amateur Radio license is not required for Associate Membership.) For more information about ARRL and answers to any questions you may have about Amateur Radio, write or call:

ARRL—The national association for Amateur Radio
225 Main Street
Newington CT 06111-1494

Voice: 860-594-0200
Fax: 860-594-0259

E-mail: **hq@arrl.org**
Internet: **www.arrl.org/**

Prospective new amateurs call (toll-free):
800-32-NEW HAM (800-326-3942)
You can also contact us via e-mail at **newham@arrl.org**
or check out **ARRLWeb** at **www.arrl.org/**

Notes

Notes

Notes

Please use this form to give us your comments on this book and what you'd like to see in future editions, or e-mail us at **pubsfdbk@arrl.org** (publications feedback). If you use e-mail, please include your name, call, e-mail address and the book title, edition and printing in the body of your message. Also indicate whether or not you are an ARRL member.

Please check the box that best answers these questions:
How well did this book prepare you for your exam?
   ☐ Very Well   ☐ Fairly Well   ☐ Not Very Well
Did you pass?   ☐ Yes   ☐ No
Where did you purchase this book?
   ☐ From ARRL directly   ☐ From an ARRL dealer

Is there a dealer who carries ARRL publications within:
   ☐ 5 miles   ☐ 15 miles   ☐ 30 miles of your location?   ☐ Not sure.

If licensed, what is your license class?＿＿＿＿＿＿＿＿＿＿＿＿＿＿＿＿＿＿

Name ＿＿＿＿＿＿＿＿＿＿＿＿＿＿＿＿＿＿＿＿＿＿＿＿＿＿＿   ARRL member? ☐ Yes ☐ No
＿＿＿＿＿＿＿＿＿＿＿＿＿＿＿＿＿＿＿＿＿＿＿＿＿＿＿ Call Sign＿＿＿＿＿＿＿
Address ＿＿＿＿＿＿＿＿＿＿＿＿＿＿＿＿＿＿＿＿＿＿＿＿＿＿＿＿＿＿＿＿＿＿＿＿＿
City, State/Province, ZIP/Postal Code ＿＿＿＿＿＿＿＿＿＿＿＿＿＿＿＿＿＿＿＿＿＿
Daytime Phone (   ) ＿＿＿＿＿＿＿＿   Age＿＿＿＿＿   E-mail＿＿＿＿＿＿＿＿＿
If licensed, how long?＿＿＿＿＿＿＿＿＿＿＿＿＿
Other hobbies＿＿＿＿＿＿＿＿＿＿＿＿＿＿＿＿＿

For ARRL use only	G Q&A
Edition	3 4 5 6 7 8 9 10 11
Printing	1 2 3 4 5 6 7 8 9 10 11

Occupation＿＿＿＿＿＿＿＿＿＿＿＿＿＿＿＿＿＿＿

From _____

_____

_____

EDITOR, THE ARRL'S AMATEUR GENERAL Q&A
ARRL—THE NATIONAL ASSOCIATION FOR AMATEUR RADIO
225 MAIN STREET
NEWINGTON CT 06111-1494

---please fold and tape---